True Connection

True Connection

Using the NAME IT Model
to Heal Relationships

George Faller and Heather P. Wright

TRUE CONNECTION
Using the NAME IT Model to Heal Relationships

All biblical references in this book come from the New Revised
Standard Version, unless otherwise noted.

Cover and interior design: Rob Dewey
Typesetting: PerfecType, Nashville, TN

Print ISBN: 978-1-5064-3177-2
eBook ISBN: 978-1-5064-3421-6

The paper used in this publication meets the minimum
requirements of American National Standard for Information
Sciences — Permanence of Paper for Printed Library Materials,
ANSI Z329.48-1984.

Manufactured in the U.S.A.

From George

To my dad, who figured out how to love me without a map, and my sons Christian (CJ) and Dylan: thanks for being such willing guinea pigs to my imperfect attempts at unconditionally loving you like your perfect Parent above.

From Heather

To my family—Mark, Douglas, Catie, and Alyse—and for my parents, Geoff and Betsy. Experiencing life together we have discovered, despite life's challenges, that as love deepens, hope grows.

Contents

Series Preface

MY MOST sincere wish is that the Living with Hope series will offer comfort, wisdom—and hope—to individuals facing life's most common and intimate challenges. Books in the series tackle complex problems such as addiction, parenting, unemployment, pregnancy loss, serious illness, trauma, and grief and encourage individuals, their families, and those who care for them. The series is bound together by a common message for those who are dealing with significant issues: you are not alone. There is hope.

This series offers first-person perspectives and insights from authors who know personally what it is like to face these struggles. As companions and guides, series contributors share personal experiences, offer valuable research from trusted experts, and suggest questions to help readers process their own responses and explore possible next steps. With empathy and honesty, these accessible volumes reassure individuals they are not alone in their pain, fear, or confusion.

The series is also a valuable resource for pastoral and spiritual care providers in faith-based settings. Parish pastors, lay ministers, chaplains, counselors, and other staff and volunteers can draw on these volumes to offer skilled and compassionate guidance to individuals in need of hope.

Each title in this series is offered with prayer for the reader's journey—one of discovery, further challenges, and transformation. You are not alone. There is hope.

Beth Ann Gaede, Series Editor

Titles in the Living with Hope Series

Nurturing Hope: Christian Pastoral Care in the Twenty-First Century
(Lynne M. Baab)

Dignity and Grace: Wisdom for Caregivers and Those Living with Dementia (Janet L. Ramsey)

Jobs Lost, Faith Found: A Spiritual Resource for the Unemployed
(Mary C. Lindberg)

They Don't Come with Instructions: Cries, Wisdom, and Hope for Parenting Children with Developmental Challenges
(Hollie M. Holt–Woehl)

True Connection: Using the NAME IT Model to Heal Relationships
(George Faller and Heather P. Wright)

Waiting for Good News: Living with Chronic and Serious Illness
(Sally L. Wilke)

Preface

WE ARE so glad you picked up our book on relationships. We hope this book helps you understand how to repair conflict, move from disconnection to reconnection, and discover God's movement in your life and relationships. From couples to families, community, and God, we outline a model for how healing happens and relationships can be transformed.

From our years of counseling individuals, couples, and families, we decided to slow down the process of reconciling to show what it looks like and describe it in micro-moves. How does change happen? We call this model for repairing and healing NAME IT (Notice, Acknowledge, Merge, Embrace, Integrate, and Thank). Change requires us to first connect with our own hearts and stories, then understand the other person's position, and finally merge those two truths (or versions of what is happening). In doing so, our deepened honesty and openness will draw out a response from the other person. The potential for change is there. Throughout the upcoming chapters, we invite you to apply this to your relationships and see what is possible. We know it works for us in our relationships and those we serve.

As coauthors, we both learn so much through the process of writing and sharing together. We bring different ideas and experiences to one another, and as "iron sharpens iron," we help each other refine our ideas and discover new and better options than either of us could come up with on our own. The process of connecting and repairing requires humility and the ability to risk, but as we find in our creative process, the results greatly outweigh the cost. Take this journey with us and see if you agree!

Acknowledgments

THERE ARE so many people behind any creative effort and many we wish to thank. We are both grateful for the opportunity to work on our second book together and that the effort really does get easier with practice.

We want to thank the Rev. Dr. Lynne Baab, who several years ago made a connection for us with the Rev. Beth Gaede. As our fearless editor, Beth pushed us to clarify what we mean and refine our focus, and asked thoughtful questions that also deepened our books tremendously. We cannot imagine working with anyone else on our combined efforts. We know the book is far better because of your input and encouragement.

Both of us work on a team at the Greenwich Center for Hope and Renewal with nine other counselors, two other staff, and a supportive board. Our shared team and supervision meetings, trainings together, and collegial support and affirmation help us both become more thoughtful and compassionate counselors and people.

We are grateful to Fortress Press for including us in their vision for the Living with Hope series and trusting it will equip many, both clergy and lay, to face life's challenges with greater meaning and resolve.

I (Heather) wish to thank my entire extended family and dear friends for loving me through the labor-intensive task of book writing. For my husband, Mark, and children, Douglas, Catie, and Alyse, thank you for standing by me, putting up with a distracted wife/mother, and letting me tell some of your stories in the book. I also want to thank my parents, Geoff and Betsy, for their willingness to let their stories be told and for teaching me what it means to grow up knowing you are loved.

I (George) wish to thank my entire support network: my friends, colleagues (both firefighters and therapists), the Emotionally Focused Therapy (EFT) community, the Faller family from College Point for teaching me the value of family, and Kathy and my boys for putting up with all my psychobabble and still wanting to spend time with me.

Finally, we both want to thank God for this opportunity, the words that came, and the inspiration to keep trying each day to love those who cross our paths with the love of Jesus Christ. To God be the glory.

1

Designed for Relationships

SO OFTEN as clergy and therapists, we are honored by the stories that come back to us. I (Heather) was presenting on loss to a large group. A gentleman raised his hand to share a story about his lifetime love affair with his wife, which extended into her last decade as a person with Alzheimer's. He shared the challenges of being a caregiver to his wife—dressing, bathing, feeding, even putting on lipstick on her. He shared that he came to understand her increasing limitations and find ways to work with them. One routine with her continued to her last day, even when she had to spend the last five years in a skilled nursing facility. He would arrive and announce in a glad voice, "Ellen, I'm here for my kiss." Despite the quiver of emotion in his voice, he smiled broadly describing how his wife puckered up her lips from bed every time he arrived for his visit. Love transcends losses, even those of our cognitive functions. When he finished speaking, there wasn't a dry eye in the room.

Love impacts and inspires us all, yet understanding what it is and how it works often leaves us all confounded.

What is love, really? We know love when we see it, like in this story, and we all long for a loving relationship that has such enduring beauty and tenderness. Love impacts and inspires us all, yet understanding what it is and how it works often leaves us all confounded.

As complicated as life and love can be, God has a simple plan to make it all manageable: the circle of life. This loop from life to death and back to life is found everywhere, from the smallest molecules to vast solar systems. Nature, energy, continuously moves through three states: (1) connection (life), when different elements work together harmoniously; (2) disconnection, when a failure to join typically results in tension, fighting, or stagnation (death); and (3) repair, moving from disconnection back to connection (rebirth).

All of existence, including human relationships, follows this same pattern. Look around, and you will notice humans are not so different from the birds flying or the tree in which they build their nest. A flower blooming today dies tomorrow and turns into the mulch and fertilizer necessary for its seeds to live and replace it. There is an economy of grace in this circle of life, because all three elements—life, death, and rebirth—are essential to continued growth and development.

Obviously, relationships are central to the function of all creation, and connection is the good stuff all organisms strive to achieve. Think about the best moments in your life: your first kiss, the birth of a child, a meaningful conversation, or an inspiring sunset in an exotic setting. They all share a felt sense of connection. Another word for the state of connection is love. Love is the energy holding everything together. This invisible force of love is operating everywhere. Because humans are made in God's image, love is the most important raw material of our lives.

Although love is challenging to define and takes on different forms in different relationships (love of partner, child, friend, country, God, things, activities, and so forth), it's a state we all experience. Love makes us feel good, in sync, open, alive, safe, curious, creative, inspired, passionate, attuned, trusting, and joined in the present moment. Connection is the whole point of life. God's design for love is for it to be a constant state of reciprocal flow between people giving and receiving. In this dynamic exchange, we need to pour ourselves out to make room to receive, and in receiving we have more to give. Higher degrees of active sharing translate into robust connections, while poor engagement leads to distance and disconnection.

Life, death, and rebirth are essential to continued growth and development.

Inevitably, people cannot perpetually stay in a state of connection. Something comes along that breaks connection, leading to feelings of hurt, disappointment, fear, pain, loneliness, unfairness, anger, sadness, helplessness, and hopelessness. These negative feelings are our body's signal that something is wrong. If the disruption to connection can be repaired, then it is no big deal. However, if the disconnection is prolonged, then we are set up for chronic isolation. Most of today's mental, physical, emotional, and spiritual ailments are directly linked to disconnection.

Still, science is discovering that disruptions are not always bad; in fact, they are necessary for our survival and growth. For organisms to thrive, they need to be open and adjust to feedback from their environment. Otherwise they do not change, and the lack of feedback leads to stagnation and apathy. Relationships are like our muscles: they need a work out and to stretch to grow otherwise they wither away. It turns out to achieve the best connections, we all need a little bit of disconnection, fighting, and distress. There can be no true union without separation, no return home without leaving.

Often, disconnection is just a sign telling us we need to do something differently. Disconnection provides necessary, healthy information to correct our course and adjust our ways. Striving for a perfect relationship devoid of any disconnection is impossible and certainly guarantees only inertia and futility. Learning to embrace the opportunity in disconnection is a much healthier response than believing the disconnection is proof the relationship is failing. Often, the beautiful gift of connection arrives wrapped in the ugly packaging of disconnection.

The crucial factor in transforming disconnection into connection is the ability to repair. A successful repair improves upon what needs fixing and brings people back into connection again. Unsuccessful repairs lead to further disconnection and pain. In relationships, true repair isn't trying to return people to the connection they had prior to the rupture. Rather, it's trying to create a new relationship through the growth caused by the changes of the disconnection.

> These negative feelings are our body's signal that something is wrong.

God's love loop is so vibrant and resilient because all three parts—connection, disconnection, and repair—are absolutely critical to our well-being. Take away any of the three, and the loop is incomplete. When the loop is complete, the repair from disconnection to connection is trying to get people back not to the "old normal" of their relationship but to a new destination that is always unfolding with new possibilities. Real connection is never boring because it is forever changing and full with the excitement of unlimited potential.

Enjoying the fruits of relationships and becoming part of something bigger than ourselves is at the very core of our existence. Let's explore love and the factors that bring us a greater sense of life, vitality, and spiritual purpose.

What Is Love?

Turns out defining love is not so easy. Looking for the answer to this question consistently ranks on Google among the highest search requests every day. For ages, the quest to define love has been championed by philosophers, poets, scientists, religious scholars, and many others. Although the answers seem endless, we believe love is simply our need to connect. We are designed to constantly be in multiple relationships simultaneously. We must relate in families, with friends, in small groups, in large communities, with nature, with our environment, with God, and with ourselves. We all share a common starting point of being born into connection, and we all share a mutual destiny of returning to connection with God when we die.

Think about our ancestors, trying to survive against saber-toothed tigers and a hostile environment. Lacking speed, size, large teeth, or claws, we seemed doomed for extinction. Yet, our abundant shortcomings were compensated for by our greatest gift: our ability to connect and work together. Getting along with others to pool resources, to offer support and mutual defense, is as essential to our survival as food, shelter, and oxygen. In fact, human brains grew as

Love is simply our need to connect.

our social group expanded. Today, scientists have discovered that the strongest predictor of a species' brain size is the size of its social group.[1] The whole point of a big brain is to help us navigate the complexities of connection.

The significance of relationships can't be reduced to a healthy "want" that enriches our lives. Rather, relationships are a fundamental "need" if we are to exist. Babies deprived of human contact, even though their physical needs for food and water are met, not only fail to thrive, they literally die. Our nervous systems are created to connect, and when they fail to connect with another they wither away. We must bond with others; that is our nature.

This longing for others is planted in our hearts and is the only truly healthy addiction. The reward centers in our brain crave interaction and fire off with delight when their need is met. We are not supposed to go without connection. When we fail to bond in healthy ways through relationships, we will bond with a faulty substitute: food, drugs, alcohol, gambling, porn, television, smart phones, or social media. There is no denying the truth that we are going to bond to something; our choice is what we decide to bond to.

The key to healthy bonding is forming a relationship with someone who is available and responsive, which creates a sense of security, trust, and understanding. Knowing there is someone to depend upon makes it easier to explore the world. In the presence of another, we can celebrate the victories and receive comfort in the pain of defeat. Having the freedom to choose who to engage with and invest our time and energies in is risky because what if the person we choose to relate to is unresponsive? No one can be forced to open their hearts to love. One could argue that we can be made to perform certain actions, but the decision to give oneself in love is always voluntary. That is what makes the other person's response so magical. They freely made a decision to come forward and engage. Love yearns for participation and longs to be seen, heard, felt, needed, and desired. At the end of our days, our

There is no denying the truth that we are going to bond to something; our choice is what we decide to bond to.

accomplishments and accumulations matter much less than the connections we formed with those we love. The freedom of love transcends time and space. We believe love is the very thing we carry over into life after earth.

In all types of relationships, it is the active nature of love that awakens the heart, unleashing passion, creativity, exploration, and amazement. Love doesn't care about last year or tomorrow; it is alive in the moment. Talking, listening, embracing, and kissing are all responses to the now. When we are in sync with someone, the connection is like we share a brain and body. In a deep conversation, it is common for one person to finish the other person's sentences, because their nervous systems are literally linked. Scientists demonstrate how people's brain waves, heart rates, and bodily responses coordinate and create a shared rhythm. If we listen, our hearts, minds, and bodies will send us clear signals of love working.

The proof of connection is found in feelings of happiness, joy, excitement, playfulness, elation, warmth, calmness, peacefulness, lightness, safety, trust, harmony, satisfaction, empathy, and affection. In love, the body expects the positive and doesn't worry about the negative. When we are in the zone of connection with another, our body keeps score by sending clear signals of positive affect. All we need to do is check the scoreboard to tally up the good feelings versus the negative feelings to see if we are succeeding at the game of love. This takes the guesswork out of the mystery of love. If the bond is strong, the body tells us everything we need to know.

I (George) remember walking on the beach with my one-year-old son CJ, when he stopped and pointed up to the sky and said, "Bird." It was his first word, and I was awestruck. In this simple moment, we joined together to enjoy a bit of wonder. The sparkle in his eyes and smile on his face were contagious. I beamed with delight and wanted to stretch out that amazing moment for eternity. I stood their grinning until the same bird flew over and pooped on CJ's head, replacing the smile with tears. To get back to smiles

> The proof of connection is found in feelings of happiness, joy, excitement, playfulness, elation, warmth, calmness, peacefulness, lightness, safety, trust, harmony, satisfaction, empathy, and affection.

and to celebrate the milestone, we bought some ice cream, because everyone knows ice cream makes everything better.

What Does the Heart Have to Do with Love?

For centuries, the word love has been intimately linked to the heart. To discover love, Cupid is aiming for the heart, not a headshot. Paying closer attention to our heart reveals how central it is in understanding connection. The heart is like a GPS for relationships. It is much more than a pump. Science is supporting poets by demonstrating that the heart is actually a highly complex, self-organizing information-processing center that functions like a second brain. The heart's neural circuitry enables it to act independently of the upper brain to learn, remember, make decisions, and feel.[2] The brain-heart connection isn't a one-way street where the brain sends commands down to the heart; rather, both organs reciprocally respond to and affect each other's functioning.

Listening to both the heart's intuition and the brain's insight helps us speak our needs directly. Honest words said in love can lead to a mutual and responsive relationship. The heart constantly assesses how we are relating to those around us and provides immediate information about how the relationship is doing. Is your heart racing with fear or growing cold from the distance of disconnection? Or is your heart jumping with joy or radiating the calmness of connection? Listening to the heart's signals empowers us to flexibly adjust to the changing needs of relationships.

To better understand our heart's signals, it is useful to know about the hormone oxytocin, also known as the "cuddle" or "love" hormone. The purpose of oxytocin is to help us stay calm while it primes us to connect with others for support. The warm feeling of oxytocin released during connections such as holding a child, seeing an old friend, or making love to your partner is evidence of a connection working well. Certainly, oxytocin is critical to any connection, but what most people don't realize is oxytocin is also

The heart is like a GPS for relationships.

essential in disconnection. During the fight-or-flight response to stress and disconnection, the body releases cortisol and adrenaline to mobilize action. Yet, the body also releases oxytocin, trying to encourage us to take action *with others*, to not fight or flee alone. Especially in times of distress, awareness of our need to connect is essential to enduring the distress. Oxytocin increases our ability to read social cues, empathize with and understand others, and figure out our own needs. Oxytocin is always pushing us to repair and turn the disconnection into connection. Interestingly, the part of our body responsible for producing the most oxytocin isn't the brain but the heart, providing strong evidence that the heart is truly the home base of love.

Most of us know the feeling of being high on oxytocin. Picture your first date or your wedding day. Just the memory elicits positive feelings and big smiles. While I (George) was dating Kathy (my future wife), we took a camping trip across the country. I concealed an engagement ring inside my wallet and planned on "popping the question" at our final destination, Yellowstone Park. Two days away from Yellowstone, we stopped for gas. As I pumped, Kathy paid the attendant inside. When she got back to the car, she said, "Here's your wallet" and placed it on the car roof. Well, as you can imagine, I never heard her (a sign of things to come in our marriage), and we drove off. When we arrived at our campsite and I asked for the wallet, she reminded me she had left it on the roof of the car for me. I turned white. We jumped back into the car and retraced our route, going way over the speed limit. I can still today see the image of a small black dot in the dirt road with dollar bills blowing alongside. I threw the car in park and, disregarding the blowing bills, raced to pick up the wallet. It had been run over by a truck, and as I felt the ring, I knew it was bent. But at least the diamond was strong.

Two long days later, at sunrise, I handed Kathy a box of Cracker Jacks with the ring at the bottom. Her surprise was complete, and I still get goosebumps thinking about her tears of joy. When I asked Kathy to marry me, her yes made my heart dance with delight. Like my son's first word, there is something transcendent when two

The purpose of oxytocin is to help us stay calm while it primes us to connect with others for support.

Being in connection with another is the homeland of our hearts and souls.

True union does not erase distinctions but actually intensifies them to create more harmonious diversity. The more one gives one's self in creative union with another, the more one becomes one's self. This union is mirrored in the Trinity: perfect giving and perfect receiving among three who all remain completely themselves.

people merge to experience something neither can find separately. We both were high on oxytocin, and the power of that moment was so intense that even all these years later the memory still unleashes waves of elation. That's the beauty of connection. It surpasses time and place. Being in connection with another is the homeland of our hearts and souls.

God's Perspective on Love

Love is expansive. When we risk opening our heart to love, we paradoxically come closer not only to someone else but also to ourselves and the world. We experience love in that place in each of us where longing and desire reside. Longing reaches both outward and deeper inward. We simultaneously know another and are known. True union does not erase distinctions but actually intensifies them to create more harmonious diversity. The more one gives one's self in creative union with another, the more one becomes one's self. This union is mirrored in the Trinity: perfect giving and perfect receiving among three who all remain completely themselves.

We are invited to partake of God's eternal love found in the Trinity. Theologians call this relationship between God the Father, God the Son, and God the Holy Spirit *perichoresis*—a dance among three equal, coexisting, and interdependent beings in the one Godhead. We believe our God is three-in-one, meaning all share in one essence but are known in three persons. In this interaction of the Godhead, there is an eternal, mutual, and loving relationship. This way of loving is the template for all connection based on mutually affirming, supportive, and reciprocal responsiveness. There is a constant exchange of giving and receiving in love. Love is meant to be experienced. Michael Brown writes in *The Presence Process*: "Giving and receiving is the energetic frequency upon which our universe is aligned. All other approaches to energy exchange immediately cause dissonance and disharmony in our life experience."[3] Failing to engage in this energy exchange leaves us separated from God's flow.

While the concept of the Trinity is often just beyond the edge of our comprehension, we do know those moments when our hearts are so filled with love for another that we are transported to something greater. We describe those moments of transcendence as "a taste of heaven." Knowing love in all its fullness brings a feeling of peace and joy. Our hearts find contentment, and we have that sense of homecoming to something that we were made for and only occasionally experience.

Because we are made in God's image, we are hardwired for relationships. Because we are relational at our core, connections with God and others bring us a greater sense of life, vitality, and spiritual purpose. They are positive, life-giving forces for health, growth, and transformation.

Biblical Wisdom on the Power of Relationships

In considering what relationships are meant to be, we look to the Scriptures for grounding. In our Christian faith, the Scriptures tell us that God is love, God so loved the world that God gave God's only Son, and others will know we are Christians by our love. Love is at the center of our relationship with God, because God first loved us, and love is the call of the Christian life. It is to be at the center of how we interact with others.

A Scripture passage often read at weddings defines love. 1 Corinthians 13:4–8 gives us a list of both what love is and what it isn't.

> Love is patient; love is kind; love is not envious or boastful or arrogant or rude. It does not insist on its own way; it is not irritable or resentful; it does not rejoice in wrongdoing, but rejoices in the truth. It bears all things, believes all things, hopes all things, endures all things. Love never ends.

The Scriptures are specific and insightful about what character traits and attitudes are going to cultivate growth and deepen connection. None of us desire a relationship that is marked by the opposite

Because we are made in God's image, we are hardwired for relationships.

of these claims. Let's try that out. What if the text read, "Love is not patient or kind but is jealous, boastful, and proud. It demands its own way. It is irritable and resentful, rejoices in injustice, and despairs when the truth wins out. Love gives up, loses faith and hope, and can't survive under pressure. Love ends." That sounds dismal, doesn't it? We know the power of the correct reading, how it was intended. Operating within God's design makes sense, even for people who don't have a spiritual frame of reference. We believe anyone you ask would identify the correct reading—certainly agreeing it describes what we want from the people closest to us.

Paul goes on in verse 13 of chapter 13 to tell us, "Three things will last forever—faith, hope, and love—and the greatest of these is love." Faith and hope seem so foundational that it is remarkable love gets first-place billing. Perhaps Paul knew that the only way to have hope and find faith is born out of love. The love of God for us inspires us to love God in return. "*We love* each other *because God loved* us first" (1 John 4:19). God invites us to a loving relationship. When we abide in God's love, the Spirit of God abides in us. We are invited into a mutual relationship of love and respect.

> The love of God for us inspires us to love God in return.

How are we to live out this God-inspired way of being with others in light of God's invitation? We find more answers in Colossians 3:12–14:

> Since God chose you to be the holy people he loves, you must clothe yourselves with tenderhearted mercy, kindness, humility, gentleness, and patience. Make allowance for each other's faults, and forgive anyone who offends you. Remember, the Lord forgave you, so you must forgive others. Above all, clothe yourselves with love, which binds us all together in perfect harmony.

These verses remind us of the ways we are to engage with others and what love means.

By being rooted in the love of Christ, we can be filled with the fullness of God. Life is meant to be full, abundant, like streams of living, overflowing water. That fullness can be with us, on the good days and the bad. That God is with us is a promise repeated throughout the Hebrew and Christian Scriptures: "Yea, though I walk through the valley of the shadow of death, thou art with me" (Ps 23:4 KJV).

We are never alone; nothing can separate us from God's love. Realizing this fundamental truth encourages us to follow God's example and lead with love, so "they will know we are Christians by our love." First-century Christians, as described in Acts 2, were known and respected by others outside their community for how they loved one another. Their generosity and concern for each other's welfare drew other followers, and others were saved as a result (Acts 2:47). Love in action draws us in and inspires something better in each of us as a result. Like the waves of the ocean, the call to love never ceases.

The Scriptures hold up for us an ideal. They reveal something of the heart of God, and of the love of God, to which we can aspire through the power of Christ's love at work in and through us. Not only is Christian love meant to mirror the love between the Trinity, but it also serves the function of healing lives and relationships, bringing about what our Jewish friends call *tikkun olam*, actions to better, perfect, or repair the world.

The challenge is that often we're living somewhere between love and disconnection in our relationships with our spouses, children, parents, and friends. We have not yet met a person who has not grown up with bumps and bruises along the journey of life. Things haven't gone 100 percent their way. People have let them down. At some point, they've learned what it's like to feel "unlovable."

The good news is that love can heal and restore. The work we do in counseling is often to repair those places in us that feel lost, alone, frightened, and even worthless. Those feelings often drive our sense of shame and, because we fear negative responses, can keep us away from others. Our shame and fear keep us from the very thing that will bring recovery and wholeness. We may run away from the only true source of healing, because the risk of possible rejection feels

> We are never alone; nothing can separate us from God's love.

too great and the negative tapes we've come to believe have been reinforced too often.

The power of counseling for couples and families is that they have a chance to begin to repair those places where that unlovability resides and to receive love not only from a caring counselor but also from their own loved ones, whom they take with them beyond the counseling hour. People learn to love each other differently and therefore can operate in a new way in their relationships outside the counseling office. Our job as ministers and counselors is to help people to love better and to remove the boundaries and walls that keep them from receiving love that is there for them.

In many respects, the journey from love to disconnection, to repair could also define our spiritual journeys. We begin in love, not only through the love of two humans who have decided to partner in our creation, but also in the unconditional love of our heavenly Parent. Most of us along life's journey experience a season of disillusionment, of wondering, of questions and doubts. We have that sense of unlovability, not only with human love but with divine love as well. Many of us have a hard time believing that God's love is as deep and wide and long as the Scriptures promise. So, we often keep God at arm's length, fearing judgment and condemnation or, perhaps even worse, indifference. We might also question the existence of God, even as we seek for a sense of meaning and purpose.

But these disappointments and doubts along the way can lead us back to the heart of God. Our sanctification is a process, notably of seeking and finding but also of surrender. Just like with human love, opening our hearts to God is a risky and courageous thing to do. Yet, the alternative—to not connect—denies our nature. God's promise is crystal clear: eternal life is found in love. When we remember that God, as Trinity, is eternally in a loving relationship and inviting us to participate in the same relationship, we realize we have everything to gain by accepting God's invitation.

Love can heal and restore.

The ultimate goal of this book is to help readers accept God's invitation to love. The ups and downs of life are gradually readying our souls to join in the eternal intimacy of Divine connection. We believe God is less concerned with intellectual doctrines and laws and more interested in what is burning in our hearts. As so many artists showed in the old paintings of saints with their hearts on fire, God longs for our active and passionate participation. When we are disconnected, God craves to redeem, not judge. We are the "beloved of God," and nothing we do can change how God relates to us. Unleash the song in your hearts, and fulfill your purpose of union with your Maker.

For Reflection and Discussion

We invite you to spend a moment journaling or talking with a confidant about these questions, and see what bubbles up for you.

1 Do you agree that relationships are necessary to your survival? How might you change the way you relate to others if you behaved as if this were true?

2 Do you have any addictive patterns, whether work, substances, technology, or food, that serve as a go-to substitute when dealing with relational challenges?

3 Does your connection with God feel safe to you? Do you carry a sense of "unloveability"?

4 How does knowing God loves you and will always be there for you impact how you interact with others and see yourself?

Our sanctification is a process, notably of seeking and finding but also of surrender.

2

The Mixed Blessing of Disconnection

Recently, I (Heather) and my husband went out to dinner. Despite the fact that we work in very different fields (he is a digital media and finance guy), he often makes astute comments about my world.

While we sipped miso soup, I told him, "What I am being reminded of in counseling is that relationships, particularly marriage, require work to keep them going."

He responded, "So much in life comes down to the second law of thermodynamics. Without energy and work, things will dissolve. It's entropy."

"That sounds important. Say more about this law of physics."

"Over time, with pressure and changes, all natural things will start to die, wear out, get cooler, and lose energy. We have to work against this force."

"That has a lot of implications for therapy, in our marriage, and even in our relationship to God."

Mark continued, "I believe the Devil is entropy. God is the opposite, providing organization, symmetry, and beauty."

"You sound like a theologian. What you are saying is right out of Genesis. In the beginning, the earth was in darkness, formless and void. God spoke into all that and brought order, creation, and beauty."

"There are forces in life that don't want good things for us as people and in marriage."

"I agree, things will dissolve and atrophy without work and energy put into what matters."

I was challenged by his insights and reminded not to coast on past successes or good times with my spouse, children, good friends, and family, but instead to remember all those relationships need to be cared for. Entropy is what happens if we aren't tending the garden or putting fuel in the tank. Living things and relationships need our time and attention. We need to work against entropy if we are to stay alive, growing, and well connected to others and to God.

The good stuff of connection is the green light of life, giving us permission to safely move ahead with our actions, dreams, and desires. Disconnection is the red light that inhibits the flow of connection. The world looks and feels very different from the vantage point of disconnection. Something or someone comes along and breaks a connection, leading to tension, arguing, miscommunication, anger, pain, isolation, alienation, withdrawal, depression, and shame. When there is dissonance in relationships, someone hurts us or gives us a certain look, or we find out someone has been gossiping behind our back, we feel rejected and betrayed. Our once open and free outlook on life becomes narrowed to one of survival and heaviness. It is difficult to enjoy a sunrise when you don't make the team, your partner dumps you, or you receive the dreaded phone call telling you someone close to you has died. Relational pain hurts. So, is it any wonder that most of us work out complex ways of trying to avoid it?

To your brain, there is no difference between social pain and stepping on a nail. The same region of the brain that registers physical pain responds the identical way to social disconnection. Both are threats to our well-being. The negative feelings accompanying disconnection are our brain's way of signaling that something is wrong and we need to act. Our negative emotions immediately remind us that the life flow of connection has been

The good stuff of connection is the green light of life, giving us permission to safely move ahead with our actions, dreams, and desires. Disconnection is the red light that inhibits the flow of connection.

broken. The distress of threats to our relationships ranges from minor annoyances like disagreeing about where to eat to intense agonies like Jesus expressed in his moment of separation from God, "My God, my God, why have you forsaken me?" Losing connection and enduring pain alone is horrific. Even God cries out in protest at the excruciating pain of disconnection.

From our earliest years we know the power of disconnection.

Every human being has a similar intense reaction to separation. No matter where you live on this planet, regardless of race, gender, or ethnicity, we see a universal response to disconnection. In the "still face" experiment, psychological researchers watch parents engage with babies. In the beginning, parents share a joyful connection with their babies, talking, laughing, smiling, making eye contact. Clearly the babies are amused and babbling with delight.

Then the parents are told to disengage and adopt a blank or still face, showing no expression, communicating nothing to their child. Immediately, something deep within the child recognizes a threat, and the baby's face expresses confusion and concern. The child's body mobilizes it for action, and the baby tries everything to get the parents to reengage. They make sounds, wave their arms, smile, point to things, anything to get their parents' attention back.

It is disturbing to watch the child deteriorate as their protests go unanswered and their bodies sink into distress. In less than two minutes, the babies cry, wail, turn away, lose control of their posture. They suffer the pain of disconnection. Witnessing their pain and helplessness breaks your heart. After an unbearable two minutes, the parents are encouraged to reengage and repair.

Most babies are resilient and bounce back quickly. After all, their desperate need for connection outweighs the mistrust created by the disconnection. The babies try again and are relieved to discover a pathway back to the pleasure and satisfaction of connection. Yet, their bodies remember the pain of disconnection, and their sensitivity to the future possibilities of other hurtful separations

To your brain, there is no difference between social pain and stepping on a nail.

grows with every bad experience. Even worse, imagine what it is like for babies or people who cannot find their way back to connection and get lost in their own isolated world? The two minutes of hell stretch out for a lifetime.

Our early stories shape our future ways of engaging with others.

Isabel is an example of someone who grew up in an environment of disconnection. On paper, she appears lucky, being born in a privileged, affluent house. Yet appearances can be deceiving. Isabel's parents didn't receive affection and affirmation as children, so they didn't know how to give it to Isabel. They were perfectionists who valued excellence and pushed Isabel hard to perform well. There was no talk in their house about vulnerabilities or struggles, just the bottom line: did you succeed or not? Children were to be "seen and not heard," and Isabel spent more time with tutors and nannies then her actual parents.

Isabel recalls a time when she fell out of a tree and dislocated her collarbone as guests were arriving for dinner. She told her mother at dinner about her extreme discomfort, and her mother snapped, "Will you stop complaining and sit up straight at the table?" Isabel soldiered on and corrected her behavior, pushing aside her pain to gain her mom's approval.

The next day in school, the teacher noticed Isabel looked pained and was unable to raise her arm to ask a question. After learning about her injury, she sent her to the nurse. Imagine the strength it takes to not complain about a dislocated collarbone. Isabel fully expected no one to be there for her pain and resigned herself to enduring the pain alone.

Even worse than the immediate pain we feel when other people fail to engage is that the separated individual learns to deal with all relationships based on this experience. Sadly, to endure the pain of long-term disconnection, we need to find creative ways of avoiding the hurt. The most common way to escape pain is to "dissociate" and mentally leave your body. Particularly after experiencing

Our early stories shape our future ways of engaging with others.

traumatic events, dulling or disconnecting allows us to create distance from the hurt. If no one is going to respond to Isabel's hurt, then she needs to create that distance.

Yet, this short-term solution often leads to a lifestyle of chronic emotional avoidance and a deadening of the body. Not listening to the body's signals makes it hard for a person to know what is needed for repair, and tragically our own bodies themselves become another place to experience disconnection.

For Isabel, isolation and separation weren't momentary visitors but permanent residents. As the years passed, Isabel wasn't just afraid of her parent's disapproval but also of her own body and the signals it transmitted. It is a cruel irony that a parent's failure often results in the child doing that same thing that failed to work to themselves. Isabel didn't know how to respond with empathy and compassion to her own hurt, so she either tried to push herself past it or avoid it at all costs. Both strategies replicate the pattern of isolation. If you fast-forward, it is easy to see how Isabel is set up to struggle in life. She is surrounded by negative messages, both externally and internally, that reinforce her loneliness and disconnection from herself.

When trust is violated, we certainly need and seek self-protection. That is a natural and normal response to feeling unsafe. We avoid getting close to others for fear of rejection or harm. For many people, the pain of social rejection is just the tip of the iceberg. When you go underneath the water, your internal critic is much more insidious. To survive, the only viable option seems to be to distance ourselves from our own bodies, to "numb out" and reduce the hurt.

The walls we put up to avoid future damage also prevent our own and others' attempts to bridge the distance. If you reflect on the worst moments of your life—a failure, sin, or rejection—likely you were isolated from others and were feeling negative and critical of yourself. We don't do well with hurt when we are alone. Resigning oneself to isolation is accepting a life sentence that goes against

Sadly, to endure the pain of long-term disconnection, we need to find creative ways of avoiding the hurt.

our nature. Yes, avoidance protects us from the possibility of adding additional pain, but it does so at the cost of experiencing the ultimate prize: connection. A good description of hell on earth is being cut off from others in a dark hole and hating yourself in the darkness. It's normal to want to escape pain, yet accepting disconnection is heading the opposite direction from our real home and place of healing: connection.

We recommend you don't blindly believe our words or the plethora of research on disconnection but rather you try out the "still face" experiment for yourselves.

Exercise

Choose a partner and decide who is going to share something important and who is going to listen. Set a timer for two minutes as partner A shares an emotionally meaningful experience, maybe something about their partner, family, or work. Partner B listens with interest to the story. When the two-minute bell goes off, partner B adopts a blank face, no longer participating in the storytelling. He or she stares off into space, at the floor, or at a watch but not at partner A.

Although intentionally not responding may feel cruel, remind yourself this experiment is a gift to help partner A understand their response to disconnection. Some people get angry, others get confused, some lose their words, others keep on talking. There is no correct way of responding, so partner A should try to be curious with how their body deals with disconnection.

After two minutes of the still face, listening partner B can apologize and reengage as partner A continues the story.

Take a few minutes to process the experiment. What it was like to give the still face? What it was like to receive the still face? How did the apology and reengagement feel?

Reverse roles, and repeat the exercise.

Resigning oneself to isolation is accepting a life sentence.

Honoring the Function of Disconnection

Disconnection is so destructive, so why does God make it an essential part of the circle of life? It turns out disconnections are necessary agents for change and growth. Disruptions force people to get out of their comfort zones, opening us up to new perspectives and challenges. Disconnections ensure that connections are always vibrant and adaptive. If you think about the moments of great stretch in your life, they were probably preceded by some degree of disruption. There is nothing like a good dose of disconnection to motivate change.

One Day Can Change Your Life

Prior to September 11, 2001, I (George) was living a pretty normal, uneventful life. I enjoyed the benefits of many connections with my wife, Kathy; our new baby son, CJ; our dog, Zoey; a large extended family; many good friends; and a great group of fellow firefighters. My simple and carefree world crashed and burned with the collapse of the World Trade Center. In a matter of moments, 343 firefighters, some of whom I knew well, perished. Working through the grief at Ground Zero for months, I witnessed daily acts of generosity, sacrifice, and heroism. As we all faced the mounting fears of future attacks, unprecedented media coverage, and rising health risks, we longed to get back to the days prior to 9/11. Unfortunately, there was no going back.

After 9/11, every day felt like Groundhog Day, spending twelve hours on the pile searching for bodies and then attending multiple funerals. The Fire Department of New York (FDNY) has a long tradition of everyone turning out to pay their respects for a member who has died in the line of duty. Yet, how does everyone turn out when there are four different funerals happening simultaneously? The amount of loss was unprecedented. The FDNY suffered the greatest loss of firefighters in one incident in the history of the world. At times, the sadness, helplessness, and hurt certainly felt overwhelming. I wanted a break from the misery, but there was no relief in sight. How could I enjoy my simple pleasures of life—watching a Yankees game, playing

It turns out disconnections are necessary agents for change and growth.

flag football, or going fishing—when every day I was interacting with kids who would never see their firefighter parent again? The day-to-day misery and darkness surrounded me like a suffocating blanket, and I didn't know what to do. As the despair mounted, I entertained desperate thoughts of finding any way possible out of the hopelessness. When it feels like you are drowning, giving up the fight for life starts to look like a plausible option.

Little did I know at the time, but the daily grind of feeling overwhelmed was reshaping my very existence. My prior happy-go-lucky reality was radically replaced with constant worry, uncertainty, and unrelenting hurt. I couldn't escape my whirlwind of emotions. Forced to deal with the negative feelings of disconnection and distress, my perspective and values started shifting. Fighting to find meaning and purpose in a world turned upside down became more important to me than having a good time. I learned that the solution to my pain lies in heading toward it, not trying to avoid the hurt.

Often, we don't know the power of love until we really need it in our broken places. My solo attempt at solving my own problems was failing miserably. My desperation forced me to turn outward. In the arms of my wife and close friends, I found comfort for my pain and a new awareness of God's shocking message that redemption is found not in our successes but in our failings and vulnerabilities. It is not a sign of weakness that we need help in darkness. The very point of darkness is to foster connection.

Learning to honor my pain started me on a journey of helping others to do the same. If you would have told me on September 10, 2001, that in the future I would be travelling the world teaching people how to embrace pain and vulnerability, I would have said, "You're crazy; stay off the booze." But the worst day of my life dramatically changed me for the better.

Often, we don't know the power of love until we really need it in our broken places.

Standing in a Battle for Justice

We all have stories about learning from the pain of disconnection. For me (Heather), one of my stories is about the sense of rejection and hurt that came when I lost my job from the graduate school that I had helped to found. I had spent nine years, alongside six other faculty, teaching first in Colorado and then in Seattle. We came out to the Northwest with a vision for a new kind of graduate school with a broadminded approach to engaging culture and theology.

It was an ambitious mission. Many of us gave all that we had and then some to the effort. I look back and see the cost. Three of the original members' marriages ended in divorce; mine was one of them. My spouse and I had been the only full-time-faculty-member couple. I was the only full-time female faculty member and founder.

We enjoyed external success only a few years after launch, with a move away from our position as a satellite program of another school and toward full independence. However, my tenure ended poorly at the same time my marriage came undone. Encouraged by my executive presbyter, my "bishop" in the Presbyterian church, I prayerfully filed legal action. He warned me that inaction would mean that I was morally complicit with future harm to others.

It took several years and arduous rounds of depositions with degrading questions, but in the end, I won an offer of judgment for gender discrimination and wrongful termination. I never spoke publicly about my position or what I was going through. I found in those years that although it grieved me to be misunderstood and maligned in the eyes of my former students and the school's alum, there is power in silence.

Prior to this incident, I did not see myself as someone who would rattle the cage or stand up to injustice. I was a people pleaser, trying to make everyone happy at all times, no matter the cost to myself, and a performer, wanting others to respect and value me. Filing a suit, knowing others were painting a false picture of me to those

I cared deeply about, was antithetical to who I knew myself to be. However, the people pleasing and performing were masks I had learned to put on to be "liked." They were not what I was "called" to. If anything, they disguised my deeper calling, allowing me to pretend I had it all together and didn't need anything from anyone else.

The joy in the struggle was the people God put in my life, "for such a time as this." The friends and family who rallied around me and my then two-year-old daughter were healing balm. They helped me stand, to keep going, to not give up personally or professionally. They could see justice was worth fighting for no matter the cost. They were right.

I am so grateful they had a faith in me, the cause, and God that was greater than my own. Thanks in large part to their love and support, I realized I had to surrender the need to defend myself and my case. I had to grieve the potential loss of my "good name." I needed to allow the work to be done by my attorney and trust that whatever the outcome, I was following through—for the sake of those who came after me. That was enough.

In many ways, these were some of my darkest hours—not only losing my marriage, the covenantal relationship I had understood as for forever, but also feeling misunderstood and maligned by the community that I had helped birth and the students I believed in and didn't want to disappoint. A myriad of losses piled on top of each other. But I sensed my call at that time was to not give up hope and to still believe there could be a tomorrow better than today. That was my daily prayer.

I realize looking back on that season that my people pleasing and performing had to take a back seat. They were tools of disconnection I had practiced to keep myself safe from harm, but in the end, loss and suffering found me just the same. It was only in laying those defenses down that I could realize fully the support and care of others. Disconnection led to reconnection with others who cared for me and had my well-being in mind.

Disconnection's Powerful Invitation

Disconnection motivates us to realign our values and can enrich our relationships. Good relationships in marriages, families, friendships, partnerships, groups, or teams are based on trust established by working through the good and bad times together. Bringing people together is making room for their multiple truths. Without someone challenging our views and disagreeing, we may have little motivation for growth. When we do not need to consider another's truth, the world shrinks. Relationships are a mirror showing us what we like and don't like. When we agree with others, relationships bask in the connective glow of relaxation and enjoyment. Yet, when we disagree, it is time to stretch. In joining with others, compromising to find our truth together, we find in giving to the other that we receive more in return.

Too many people in relationships don't understand disconnection. Instead of taking the opportunity to change, they double down on their truth, each insisting they are correct. They start to keep score of who is right and wrong, who is contributing more and less to the relationship, and before they know it the distance in their relationship becomes devastating. The discomfort God designed as a temporary state becomes perpetual.

Most people don't recognize that doing relationship math separately never adds up and ultimately leads to deficits on both sides. The "us versus them" (or "me versus you") mentality usually ends up in loneliness, just "us"—or "me." Living in continuous deficit turns the world into a dark and dreary place. Disconnection is an invitation for both sides to shift their stance and replace hard positions with the give-and-take of generosity and grace.

Recognizing and honoring the function of disconnection and negative reactions allows us to use their wisdom to promote change. When disconnection occurs, we are given opportunities to rebuild trust and make it even stronger than before the relational break. The key to success is seizing the opportunity of disconnection instead of

> Relationships are a mirror showing us what we like and don't like.

fighting it. Unfortunately, many people are unaware of the positive possibilities of disconnection and develop strategies to avoid it. Although this attempt to escape the pain of disconnection makes sense, it is doomed to failure. No one can avoid the circle of life.

As we (George and Heather) have grown in our clinical experience and understanding, we are determined to avoid shaming or convicting people for their chosen path for surviving disconnection. Rather, we celebrate their resourcefulness in finding a way to endure difficult situations. Like Isabel, we all do our best to survive. However, each of us faces this universal question: is the adaptive behavior of the past still needed today? Every one of us must decide, Is it time to let go of our strategies for self-protection if they are hindering us from receiving the benefits of working through disconnection right now? It is our choice to surrender to the bitterness, resentment, coldness, and isolation of disconnection or to fight to get back to our true destination of acceptance, warmth, love, and connection.

When disconnection occurs, we are given opportunities to rebuild trust and make it even stronger than before the relational break.

God Using Disconnection

We believe it is by divine purpose that we work through disconnection toward healing or repair. Heaven is a place of ultimate connection with God and one another. We know we have not arrived at heaven on earth and we are people in process, trying with limited success to reestablish our lost connection with God. Our world offers many blessings but also many crises, woes, instabilities, and uncertainties. Disconnection from God, others, and ourselves is the norm for many people. After spending so much time disconnected, we have a hard time trusting others and believing in a loving and good God.

Theologically speaking, Christians believe we live in a fallen world. We no longer live in the garden of Eden. The outcome of original sin is disconnection from God and others. How different would humanity be if Adam and Eve had known how to honor the fear

> Many of us believe God must be disappointed with us, because we are disappointed with ourselves.

and pain of their disconnection from God and had used it to head them back toward God instead of into hiding?

Tragically, they handed down to the rest of us a template for mistrusting God and turning away from the definitive source of love and comfort. The consequence of their failing is that many of us believe God must be disappointed with us, because we are disappointed with ourselves. We expect God's frown and judgment, not a loving embrace. We affirm that because "all have sinned and fallen short of the glory of God" (Rom 3:23), we therefore deserve punishment, condemnation, and disconnection.

The apostle Paul's teaching about our disconnection from God, one another, and the rest of creation is not the end of the story, however. The two great commandments, according to Jesus's conversation with the young attorney, are to love God and to love our neighbor. Unfortunately, this message is easier to say than to practice. Failing to keep the commandment to love only reinforces our fears of unworthiness and our tendencies to hide.

> It is right here and now that the "I am that I am" shows.

The good news is that the Scriptures speak precisely to that existential angst, assuring us that God is with us. Whether we are in Ezekiel's valley of dry bones, Hosea's wilderness, the psalmist's valley of the shadow of death (Psalm 23), the tombs at Gerasa, Lazarus's tomb, the garden of Gethsemane, a crucifixion hill at Golgotha, all these dismal locales have one thing in common: God is with us there. We do not need to arrive in a pleasant place, be well-groomed and dressed to our best, or have our act together. It is right here and now that the "I am that I am" shows. "I am with you; my rod and my staff shall comfort you." God often surprises us by finding us when we are lost and wooing us back into relationship, as Hosea describes God's action. Letting a truth like that sink in radically alters our view of God and ourselves, if we risk receiving it.

For Reflection and Discussion

1 Recall your earliest memory of disconnection. Were there any

strategies or patterns you adopted to make life safe? Did you seek help from others or try to deal with it on your own? How might you respond differently now?

2 Do you see any past disconnections that opened a door to future growth? What were the keys to the change? (We'll consider this topic more in chapter 3.)

3 Which of your current relationships is in a place of disconnection? How did that happen?

4 How has God met you in the places of darkness and brokenness?

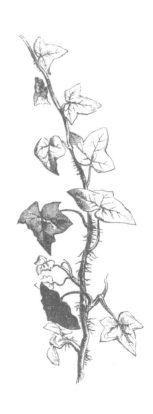

3

A Pathway to Repair

THE EXISTENTIALIST Jean-Paul Sartre, in his difficult book *Huis Clos (No Exit)*, defines hell as being trapped forever with people we don't particularly like. Our belief is that relationships, even broken ones, can be improved to enhance our lives, not diminish them or torment us. We want to show you what that repair looks like.

When our relationships feel strained or painful, we need to remember that disconnection is not the problem. Rather, what we do with disconnection determines if it leads to resiliency or demise. Disconnection is inevitable, but repair is a choice. If we do not know how to repair relationships, however, we can be stuck in extended periods of disconnection and distress, something that should frighten us all. Learning how to repair relationships empowers us to redeem the disconnection, to return to the vibrancy of the relationship. Courage, authenticity, and vulnerability are the raw materials necessary to turn the negativity of disconnection into the joy of connection.

Courage, authenticity, and vulnerability are the raw materials necessary to turn the negativity of disconnection into the joy of connection.

The only real difference between the best and worst relationships is this ability to repair. We all know of relationship endings that are heartbreaking. We often wonder if repair was possible. Sadly, not knowing how to bridge the gap in distressing relationships typically leads to resignation and further disconnection. Why bother trying to repair if talking just results in more fighting? As disconnection mounts, it robs people of hope that the distance can be bridged and their needs met. So many people believe their relationships ended when they fell out of love, when in truth it wasn't a lack of love but not knowing how to repair that did the pair in.

If you ask most people who get separated or divorced what happened, they will say the relationship broke down because of the laundry list of stuff: money, kids, work, sex, stress, addictions, infidelity, and so forth. Sadly, they are missing a deeper truth. Certainly, the countless issues triggered disagreement and tension, but what doomed the relationship was the resulting distance and mistrust. Distance is unavoidable; it's the ability to recognize and repair it that determines the outcome. Many people who learn how to repair look over their past relationships and wonder how differently things could have been if they had known this earlier. It is common at trainings we provide on repair for participants to break down in tears when they realize their previous relationships could have ended very differently.

How to Repair

Our approach can be used in any situation—between intimate partners, parents and children (for more on this, see chapter 5), siblings, friends, coworkers, neighbors, and among people of all ages. The depth of the relationship and what is hoped for will dictate how hard you work at the repair.

Research about couples shows that almost 70 percent of their problems are never resolved. Partners have different styles and are often complete opposites. If Mary is extroverted, spontaneous, fun, creative, not so organized, and usually running fifteen minutes late, then chances are her husband, Bill, is introverted, methodical, responsible, serious, and running fifteen minutes early. These two are set up to have the same fight over their different timing thousands of times. How many times is Mary going to say, "You need to loosen up a little" while Bill returns, "You need to be more reliable." Their timing incompatibility is never going to be resolved; rather, they need to learn how to live with two truths. The problem with trying to talk our partner into doing something our way is that we are trying to enforce our version of reality and the other person feels shut down and unheard. If Mary became just like Bill, the

Disconnection is inevitable, but repair is a choice.

couple might never fight about being on time but at the cost of losing so much creativity and fun. If Bill conformed to Mary's way, the couple would be an exciting train wreck. They need each other to provide checks and balance.

Yet, it is impossible to find balance when we cannot repair. Defensiveness in relationships can entrench individual positions while discounting or demonizing the other partner's stance. Before long, saying no to each other becomes the norm. As the no's mount and the distance increases, it gets harder and harder to understand your partner's world. Feeling disconnected, most of us believe we must choose between two bad options: try to talk our partner into doing something differently (not likely to succeed, as giving advice is effective only 5 to 10 percent of the time) or say nothing at all and try to avoid making things worse. Both scenarios exacerbate disconnection. People in relationship need help turning their no's into yes's.

In the hope of helping our readers learn and remember the deceptively simple process of repair, we came up with the acronym NAME IT. We believe these words can organize and facilitate change to mend our challenged relationships. As we describe the model, we invite you to consider a relationship in your life that needs some repair. Here is the NAME IT process of repair.[1]

Notice

Notice you have a disconnection, what is happening for you, and explicitly state your intention to start the repair process.

The first step to mending is recognizing there is a problem. So many of us get overwhelmed by the busyness of our lives that we fail to realize the insidious threat of miscommunication, distance, and mistrust in our relationships. We develop tunnel vision, failing to see others in our lives. It is impossible to repair if we first don't recognize and mobilize to address the issues. Choosing to confront the distance initiates the repair process.

The NAME IT
Process of Repair

N — Notice

A — Acknowledge

M — Merge

E — Embrace

I — Integrate

T — Thanks

The easiest place to begin the repair process is trying to understand your own perspective more clearly and taking responsibility for your contribution to the problem. To help gain clarity, ask yourself the following question, "How do I feel right now about my relationship?" Our feelings provide a wealth of information about what is important to us and what is happening right now. You might feel frustrated, angry, criticized, annoyed at being treated unfairly, not heard, or simply misunderstood.

Once you have identified what you feel, next ask yourself, "What do I want to do with these feelings? Do I keep them to myself, or do I express them to my partner?" There are two standard ways of protecting ourselves from the hurt of disconnection: we either push to talk or we retreat to avoid making things worse. We all do some of both, but in most relationships, people tend to fall into patterns: one pushes and the other retreats, both push, or both withdraw. Those who push are hoping to encourage the other to engage. Those who avoid talking hope their attempts to avoid conflict will calm their partner down. Both strategies provide immediate short-term protection at the cost of creating long-term relational mistrust. Figuring out and naming your preferred method for handling disconnection is crucial to repair.

After identifying your typical actions, now it is time to go deeper and ask yourself, "What do I really want?" We all have the same needs in relationships: to be seen, wanted, chosen, cherished, comforted, respected, and loved. If I want love and closeness, I need to decide if my actions are helping me get what I really want. Is my anger, frustration, and criticism or my avoidance, minimizing, and dismissing getting me closer to or further from my heart's desires? Truly taking into account—Noticing—the good reasons you protect yourself the way you do and the dismal results this strategy produces force us to consider new approaches.

We recommend a counterintuitive move. Instead of covering up your vulnerable feelings—your hurt, fear, sadness, failure, rejection,

How do I feel right now about my relationship?

What do I want to do with these feelings?

and loneliness—with defensive moves like getting angry, blaming your partner, supposedly not caring, or running away, we want you to risk staying present with the vulnerable feelings. Ironically, the way to heal our pain lies in heading toward it and listening to what it has to say, because embedded in our pain is information about what we need from our partner.

What do I really want?

Identifying our core needs is essential to shifting the communication away from reactivity and toward responsiveness. We all get creative in how we try to hide and limit our insecurities, but what gets lost in our protection is the solution: support and comfort. The tragedy of disconnection is these vulnerable feelings get "snuffed out." If we don't ask for our needs to be responded to, then "not asking results in not getting."

Sadly, the timing is terrible because precisely at our moment of greatest need, when we are feeling the most vulnerable, no one sees us and therefore no one comes to truly meet us. The more no one shows up, the harder it is to risk revealing vulnerability. To reverse this feedback loop of protection, we need to face our vulnerabilities instead of avoiding them. The Notice step is complete when you can recognize both your protective strategies and the underlying vulnerabilities that drive the need for protection.

Not asking results in not getting.

Picture a busy person taking a moment to stop their activities, look in the mirror, and reflect on their experience of the relationship.

Acknowledge

Acknowledge your partner's reality and separate truth.

A dualistic perspective holds only one truth, "I'm right and you are wrong." This either/or thinking pushes for winners and losers. In dualistic conversations, there are lots of "buts" and plenty of blame to go around. Developing a nondualistic perspective is critical to repair. Expanding to a nondualistic perspective shifts the frame to include two different realities. Typical nondualistic conversations are characterized by lots of "both of us" or "we," and the "buts" are replaced with "ands." Feel the difference between these two sentences: "I know you are angry but so am I" or "We are both angry for good reasons." Taking turns talking about how neither perspective is wrong allows each partner to be open to the other's experience.

Merging different perspectives can be done with groups of people, but since most often this is done in dyads, with two people in conversation, sometimes with the help of a minister or therapist, we are describing it dyadically. The person (partner A) who initiated the repair process in the Notice step now tries to understand partner B's moves, which we define as their position or point of view, which are often very different from his own.

The key word in this step of Acknowledge is curiosity. Partner A might not understand the moves of partner B, but curiosity starts with trust that partner B has good reasons for her thoughts, feelings, and behaviors. The same questions partner A asked himself in the Notice step are now helpful to ask partner B. What are your feelings about the relationship? What do you do with these feelings? What do you really want in this relationship? Do your protective moves help move you closer to what you want or move you further away?

As partner B starts to explore her reality and to let partner A into her version of the truth, the couple has more common ground to work with. It is important to note that the goal of this step is to expand awareness and provide greater understanding. This is not the time to get into content, details, or logistics. Partner A wants to grasp partner B's protective moves and the vulnerabilities underlying them. When partner A understands and Acknowledges partner B's experience, the couple moves on to the next step.

The partners now really see each other and turn to face the divide that separates them.

Curiosity starts with trust that partner B has good reasons for her thoughts, feelings, and behaviors.

Merge

Merge two truths to unite against the negative cycle.

Partner A recognizing partner B's truth creates the momentum necessary to now help partner B understand partner A's truth. While the moves may be different, the underlying vulnerabilities are similar. As both people acknowledge two different truths, they create awareness of how each partner's attempts to protect himself or herself reinforces the other partner's need for self-protection. They might notice a pattern such as this: if the relationship is threatened and partner A deals with threat by getting anxious and wanting to talk while partner B deals with threat by trying to minimize and not talk, then every time partner A pushes to talk it increases the likelihood partner B shuts down. And every time partner B avoids conversation, it increases the likelihood partner A will push to talk.

When you each walk in the other person's shoes, their moves make sense. Partner A pushes in the hope of increasing engagement and decreasing anxiety, because talking works for him. Yet, when you understand how partner B operates, pushing doesn't increase engagement. Quite the contrary, it increases disengagement. On the other hand, withdrawers hope the avoidance of conflict will defuse the situation because that is their go-to move. However, when you understand partner A's world, avoiding talking doesn't decrease anxiety; it spikes it.

All of us get caught in negative feedback loops or cycles where each one's protective behaviors trigger undesired responses in the other. Identifying the negative feedback loop enables people to work together instead of against each other. This shift in tying together two truths to unite for each other and against the cycle is a major accomplishment of the repair process. Both partners realize they have the same answer to the question of what they really want underneath their different defensive moves (in the Notice and Acknowledge steps of the NAME IT model): to get along better and feel closer together.

As each partner accepts responsibility for how their protective moves don't work for the other, more safety is created and each can go deeper into their vulnerable needs, which are typically hidden. Both partners begin to recognize that although their moves are different, they share the same feelings of fear, hurt, and separation underneath. For good reasons, they are both missing each other and are therefore not able to meet each other's vulnerable needs. Recognizing the different outcomes that result from protective strategies, which create distance in relationships, compared with vulnerable responsive strategies, which pull people together, empowers couples to communicate in a whole new way. Merging their two truths into a coherent narrative that explains why they miss each other sets the stage for replacing the negative cycle with a positive cycle of responsiveness. As the need to defend reduces, the longing to connect emerges.

The partners both walk across the bridge to meet in the middle, where they hold both their truths.

Embrace

Embrace the underlying vulnerabilities and empathetically respond to each other's needs, replacing the negative cycle with a positive cycle.

As partners close the gap and create safety by interrupting the negative cycle, it is time to go for the repair that transforms the misses of the negative cycle into the hits of the positive cycle. This is the riskiest part of the process, because to express our needs, we must expose our insecurities camouflaged underneath the protective strategies.

As the two shift their focus from trying to change their partner's behaviors to pay attention to their own needs, they make themselves vulnerable. Not knowing if your partner can or wants to respond is scary. If I typically express my frustration at my partner for not listening, sharing my fear that maybe my partner isn't interested in what I am saying makes me vulnerable. Or if I try to tune out my

> Both partners begin to recognize that although their moves are different, they share the same feelings of fear, hurt, and separation underneath.

> The partners both walk across the bridge to meet in the middle, where they hold both their truths.

To truly get the comfort we long for in our vulnerabilities, we must take the chance to let our partner into our dark places.

What is most important in giving and receiving forgiveness isn't saying or hearing the words "I'm sorry" but the act of looking into your partner's eyes and seeing your own pain reflected back.

partner's criticism, I take a risk when I share my fear that maybe I am failing my partner and a disappointment.

Couples wish their partners were mind readers and could anticipate what is happening and meet their needs without having to explicitly talk about vulnerabilities. Yet, we have found there is a simple rule in relationships: not asking equates to not getting. To truly get the comfort we long for in our vulnerabilities, we must take the chance to let our partner into our dark places.

By helping both parties change the level of communication away from content, defenses, logistics, and details and toward longings and vulnerabilities, the stage is set for a different outcome. Asking for comfort, reassurance, compassion, or touch is very different from getting annoyed or acting indifferent.

The research on repair reveals what is most important in giving and receiving forgiveness isn't saying or hearing the words "I'm sorry" but the act of looking into your partner's eyes and seeing your own pain reflected back. Your partner loves you enough to feel your experience with you. It is not enough to just show up and talk. You must allow your heart to be impacted by your partner's experience. As you each share fears and hurts typically hidden by your self-protection, you enable the other person to change roles from the villain to the hero.

Typically, when both people acknowledge how their well-intended interventions to fix things only made them worse, then asking for what you truly need from your partner replaces the protective feedback loop with a positive cycle of responsiveness. Good intentions are nice, but responsive actions are much better. Empathetically focusing on each other's pain and insecurities elicits healing responsiveness and active participation. You aren't just talking but encountering each other in the most vulnerable of ways. This is a sacred space where people can comfort and grow with each other. At this point of reaching toward and receiving each other's loving actions, the moment of disconnection is transformed into connection.

The partners now Embrace and comfort each other.

Integrate

Integrate the new pattern of responsiveness and celebrate the resultant positive affect.

In our experience, it is not enough to simply enjoy the Embrace and ride away together into the sunset. We need to choose and act to hold onto the new experience. Integrating reinforces positive movement in a relationship and encourages it to be repeated in the future. People need to create a narrative of how they made room for two truths and how Integrating their views allowed for greater connection. Understanding the difference between expressing vulnerabilities, which pulls people closer, versus defensiveness, which pushes people apart, is necessary for bringing about future repairs. Just like both partners worked together to create the negative cycle of defensiveness and protection, now both partners are working together to create a positive cycle of vulnerability and responsiveness.

It is very helpful to have a clear picture of what a successful repair looks like. All of us can tell a repair works when we see a shift from the negative emotions of disconnection to the positive emotions of connection. If my greatest fear is that the other person doesn't care or that I might be failing her, then expressing these fears and receiving her comfort soothes my pain. Hurt and fear give way to relief, appreciation, and joy. If there are no positive feelings experienced, then there is more distance and mistrust to work through and more repair needed. Clearly knowing physical markers to look for in the process empowers us all to stay on course. If you are not feeling better, then trust your body and realize there is more repair work to do.

The goal is connection; integrity requires that we not settle for anything less. As each person experiences the power of a dramatic shift from disconnection to connection, they create a mutual

At this point of reaching toward and receiving each other's loving actions, the moment of disconnection is transformed into connection.

The partners now Embrace and comfort each other.

Integration creates growth and strengthens the bond.

narrative that explains not only how their attempts at self-protection didn't work but, more importantly, the solution to their distance, their responsiveness. This Integration creates growth and strengthens the bond. Couples who inevitably fail together but recognize their failings open a doorway into vulnerability, where they can discover each other in a new and intimate way. They are forever emboldened to embrace the opportunity found in disconnection. Experiencing positive emotions through sharing negative, vulnerable emotions enables all of us to become experts of the repair process. Each successful repair breeds confidence and makes future attempts easier and more inviting.

The partners now create meaning for their successful repair by organizing their journey into a coherent story and deciding to move forward together with increased hope and understanding.

Thank

Thank the other person and celebrate the growth together.

To honor the repair process, it is fitting to end with appreciation. The ugliness of disconnection finds redemption in connection as the love loop comes full circle. Intentionally tying a bow on the process with a "thank you" respects the truth that we can't reach this place on our own. We are all dependent on others to reach our dreams and desires. Our progression of Notice, Acknowledge, Merge, Embrace, and Integrate ends with a Thanks as both people express their gratitude to each other with a hopeful smile or hug. It is fitting to end this repair process with mutual appreciation and celebration for the transformation of the hostility and isolation of disconnection into the magnificence of connection.

The partners finish the NAME IT process by gifting each other with words of gratitude and celebration.

The partners finish the NAME IT process by gifting each other with words of gratitude and celebration.

Our countercultural message is that we are wise to embrace disconnection and face the hurt of isolation. That embrace propels us toward the solution of repair and enables us to deal with the hurt together. NAME IT is a game plan for navigating the challenging process of repair. Each time a relationship is restored, it grows even stronger because both people involved are now more confident that breakdowns can be fixed. The pain and fighting open the doorway to healing and transformation. How exciting to realize that all the misses, defensiveness, fighting, and mis-attunement are opportunities for deeper connection for those willing to vulnerably repair. NAME IT helps couples refocus their priorities and remind each other that their relationship is more important than the problems driving them apart. Instead of fighting against each other, they shift their tactics toward fighting for each other and their relationship, and that makes all the difference.

NAME IT in Action

An example of the NAME IT process unfolding is a fight I (George) had with my sixteen-year-old son CJ last year. He was dealing with stressful schoolwork and athletic obligations by playing video games when he came home. He wasn't very engaged at home. Chores, healthy eating, manners, posture, connecting with other family members, hygiene, and sleep all took a backseat to his precious video games. The more I complained and criticized, the more he retreated, turning to his games for respite.

As a therapist, I constantly come across research decrying the evils of technology and how it is interfering with the development of empathy and our ability to read social cues. This research scares me to death. With that in mind, I was baking a salmon for dinner while, ironically, I was also scheduled to do a conference call discussing the causes of teenagers' acting-out behaviors. The dish needed thirty minutes to cook, but the call was scheduled for an hour, so I informed CJ he needed to turn off the oven after half an hour. He agreed, saying, "No problem, Dad."

When my call ended, I headed down the stairs and smelled the dinner burning. When I opened the oven door, the horribly overcooked and smoking fish gave new meaning to the term "blackened salmon." I ran

NAME IT is a game plan for navigating the challenging process of repair.

NAME IT helps couples refocus their priorities and remind each other that their relationship is more important than the problems driving them apart.

up the stairs yelling, "CJ, what happened with taking out the dinner in the oven?" As I anticipated, he was sitting at his desk playing on his computer and said, "Oh, sorry. I didn't hear you." His nonchalant attitude triggered my outrage as I shouted, "That is it! You've lost the computer for a month, and if you complain, I'm sending you away to a wilderness program where you can liberate your mind from the addiction of that damn computer!"

As expected, CJ took the bait and started protesting how unfair I was acting, saying, "I wished I lived in another house where my parents were cool and not living in the 1950s." I promptly replied, "One more comment and we'll make it two months." CJ turned off his computer and closed the door, ending another wonder day in the Faller house.

That night lying in bed, I initiated the NAME IT process by trying to Notice the problem (How could I not? I couldn't fall asleep!) and my truth about my role in the growing distance. My mounting frustrations were really about my fears for his future and my failure as his parent. Yet, I wasn't expressing any of my vulnerabilities, only my frustrations and criticisms of his behavior. I was hoping my criticism would be a good motivator. Turns out my good intentions weren't working. Despite my good reasons to push, I had to admit my efforts were ineffective.

With clarity on my truth, I decided it was time to understand CJ's world (Acknowledge). The next day after school I asked CJ to go on a walk with me so we could talk. I started off the conversation by making explicit the elephant in the room, the distance in our relationship, by saying, "Hey, pal, I know we are both crazy busy, and it seems like we are rarely getting a chance to spend any fun time together. Do you agree?" CJ shrugged his shoulders and responded with a "Yeah, I guess so."

Trying to resist the urge to get defensive, I said, "I'm hoping we can get closer again and stop all this bickering. You are a great son, and I miss spending time enjoying each other instead of fighting." CJ, nodding his head, said "Me too" but then continued, "It's hard to believe you think I'm a good son when all you do is criticize me."

In this moment, I had two options: disagree and try to get him to understand my position or get curious about his perspective. Focusing on my desire to bridge the distance, I chose to lean into his perspective by saying, "Okay, tell me more about how I criticize you." CJ described how despite being on the high honor roll and starting on the football team, all I did was express my disappointment over a million different things. I constantly tell him he doesn't brush his teeth right, doesn't pick up his clothes, doesn't read enough books, or go outside often enough. My relentless message was that he was lazy and doing it wrong. CJ didn't want to be around that negative vibe and enjoyed the "no pressure existence" video games provide. Going into his room was his way to recharge to face the stresses of the next day.

I had to admit that listening to his perspective helped me to understand the function of his withdrawal into video games. I said, "Wow! I didn't know the games helped so much. No wonder you like playing them. If I could get away from the bad to have a little fun, I'd want to do it too." CJ, with a surprised look on his face, said, "Okay, what did you do with my dad?" I laughed and replied, "Seriously, I think if I were in your shoes, I'd want to get away from the nagging too. Thanks for sharing." CJ responded with a joking, "You're welcome."

With insight into CJ's reality, it was now time to Merge our different realities into a feedback loop that helped make sense of our well-intentioned attempts at self-protection, which created distance in our relationship. Ironically, CJ started this step when he said, "I really don't get why the computer bugs you so much." I replied with a shrug, "Well, I guess I see the computer as something that interferes with your healthy development. Your brain is at its creative height, and if you don't use your neural pathways to learn new things, then those pathways shrink and die. The computer feels to me like wasted time that may also be harmful." CJ yawned and shook his head helplessly, saying, "So you push me to not be on the computer so I can do more stuff? Can't you see how I'm already maxed out?"

Together we both began to recognize our negative cycle: I try to motivate and correct his behavior with comments that actually just reinforce his need for retreat. When I understand CJ's world, criticism doesn't elicit engagement; rather, it increases the likelihood of withdrawal. On the other side of the coin, CJ is hoping that by tuning out my nagging, it will go away. Yet when he understood my concerns, he realized tuning me out only feeds my distress and my pushing increases. We both recognized the good reasons for our protective strategies were driving us further apart. Thankfully, in making this negative cycle explicit, we started bridging the distance and heading toward each other.

As the defensiveness reduced and the conversation started going deeper, we had an opportunity to make more room for our vulnerabilities underneath the protection (Embrace). CJ shared that although he tried hard to tune out the criticism, it often stuck. With sadness in his eyes, he described feeling "bad about myself, like I'm failing you as a son." His pain pulled at my heart. All I typically saw in our fights was his annoyance, never his hurt. I thought he really didn't care. Seeing his pain, I reached over and hugged him, saying, "I'm sorry, CJ. I don't even know what to say. I'm just glad you told me. I'll do a better job of showing you how much I love and am proud of you." It is easy for a parent to respond to their child's pain when the signals are clear. CJ received my response by sinking into my hug and saying, "I love you too, Dad."

It is amazing to see how in a place of connection, we are much more open and curious about the other person's experience. When CJ is feeling safe and not pressured, he is much more engaged. After our awesome hug, we continued walking, and CJ surprised me by commenting, "I think I understand your concern about my playing too much video games, but your anger happens so quickly. I don't really understand why you get so mad."

CJ's question caused me to reflect more deeply on my own vulnerabilities and touch the part of myself that feels rejected when he chooses the game over spending time with me. Allowing myself to feel the hurt underneath my pushing, I shared, "I guess it sometimes feels like you'd rather be with your computer than hanging with me. I know you've got your own life, but I miss my buddy." CJ, looking at me with compassion in his eyes, said, "I had no idea you felt bad. I just thought you were pissed off all the time. I miss hanging with you too. Let's figure out how to do a better job being with each other." I smiled, appreciating the power of connection and the love of my son.

On our way home, we jokingly organized our experience and attempted to Integrate this new level of communication. I said, "Wow, this was a pretty deep talk and we did it differently this time. I appreciate that although we have different moves, underneath we both are feeling pretty similar: alone and bad. It is incredible how sharing our deeper feelings brought us closer together instead of reinforcing our old pattern of distance. All this vulnerability stuff, I think I need a break. Maybe play some Black Ops [a video game]?" CJ laughed and said, "If we play together, does that count as quality time?'" I replied with a chuckle, "Absolutely." As we walked into our house, I expressed my Thanks and said, "Hey, I appreciate you taking the time to chat with your old man." CJ turned, sharing a huge grin, and replied, "That went much better than I thought it would."

This story highlights the key moves of the NAME IT process of repair. There is a road map to handling disagreements, although each situation is unique, so you need flexibility and patience to find the right way to repair with those you love. The key is to capture the spirit and power of holding two truths and finding connection in the space between. Turning the red light of disconnection into the green light of connection happens when we honor and recognize our longings are stronger than our fears. Being able to repair helps to reorder the disorder of disconnection and use it to create warmth, calmness, safety, and love.

Following God's Image of Repair

We know stories of repair when we hear them. As counselors and ministers, we often realize it requires a Higher Power to intervene so people can trust in a God and a sense of justice and mercy bigger than themselves—so they can have the grace to forgive, to risk again, to be open to the other. No matter how many couples we have worked with over the years, we are always humbled when the first person decides to lay down their emotional weapons and lean in to the other's experience. To really listen and to not self-defend is a heroic and courageous act, particularly when we are wounded or frightened. In every case, as we remember those we have witnessed in the past, our eyes well up with tears recalling those stories. Repair is palpable.

There are times when the people we love do things we cannot imagine or that anger us. For the parent or spouse who can lean in rather than just experience their own irritation, frustration, or disgust, amazing movement can happen, both in themselves and in the one they love. Parents and spouses who have used the steps of NAME IT can say to their loved one, "If you have to face possible ridicule or shame, you don't do it alone. I am going with you." Jesus provides us with an example of love in action. When Jesus met the woman at the well, she was shocked to find he knew her whole story yet still cared for her and offered her living water. The outcast or wrongdoer is known, in the good, bad, and ugly aspects of what one has had to face, and is loved in the midst of one's brokenness. That is when we know love is real.

Repair is seeing our faults and vulnerability and leaning into it and not away from it. It would be so much easier to walk away, get angry, or put up a wall of silence than risk stepping into another's story, especially one that is damaging to the relationship. Repair is possible when neither one gives up on the hope that this disconnect can be dealt with bravely and better.

We know stories of repair when we hear them.

Theologically, repair is about redemption, a theme found throughout the Hebrew and Christian Scriptures. Restoration, wholeness, reintegration, and finding what was lost are all definitions for redemption. When there has been a violation and breach that may seem insurmountable, miraculously another way appears. It started in the garden with Adam and Eve. After disobeying God and suffering the consequences, their Creator God took pity on their newly discovered shame at their own nakedness and clothed them in animal skins (Gen 3:21). Despite what had been done and losing the intimacy of sharing the garden with God, there was still mercy, provision, and care. God's love continued despite the punishments that were given. Sadly, the worst part of the original sin wasn't the action of biting the apple but the hiding that came afterward. Instead of heading toward God and repair, Adam and Eve headed away, toward disconnection. God created us to be in constant relationship, and this original sin introduced the pain of separation. Repair is about reconnecting what was never meant to be separated.

Later in Genesis we read of the account of Joseph. He went from being the favored son to being tossed in a pit, enslaved, falsely accused of adultery, and imprisoned, and then later made number two in the mighty land of Egypt. His broken relationships with his jealous brothers came full circle with them asking for his help and him granting them pardon and blessing. No matter what was lost and how long we have been without it, God can redeem, renew, and even make up for lost time. That is reassuring to us as therapists in our work with others. We know that God can take the most broken, troubled, and heartsick stories and weave a tapestry of beauty out of them.

Biblical Images for the Repair Process

We read about God replacing our heart of stone with one of flesh in Ezekiel 36, right before Ezekiel's vision of the valley of dry bones, a tremendous resurrection story in chapter 37. These stories remind us that in disconnection from God, ourselves, and others, we often

Theologically, repair is about redemption. Repair is about reconnecting what was never meant to be separated.

feel like stones—numb, angry, or hard-hearted. Our emotional and spiritual vitality is sapped. In the midst of that alienation, God can breathe new life, restoring life to what has been dead.

For God's people, exile periods were times of disconnection *and* times of holding out hope for revival, restoration, and return to their land and their temple to worship God as they were called to do. Exiles, wilderness periods, invite all of us to move toward reconciliation and repair. God is about making all things news. What is the place of wilderness in your life? Where might there be a door for grace to enter and make new what may have become stone in you?

In order to get to repair, we need to be willing to surrender "an eye for an eye and a tooth for a tooth" and explore what it means to turn the other cheek. We are invited, in the footsteps of Christ, not to retaliate but to offer grace. Repair isn't only about couples or families but can happen in all relationships, including within communities and between organizations. I (Heather) recently heard a story about a church trying to better understand the LGBTQ community. They held workshops on the topic, which came to the attention of some LGBTQ activists, who showed up to protest. When the workshop started, the church group welcomed everyone, especially their LGBTQ participants. In the opening prayer, the speaker prayed for forgiveness for how Christians had treated their LGBTQ brothers and sisters. The mood shifted; this was not the message the activists had expected to hear. The speaker asked if all those present would allow him to share a short address, and then he wanted to hear from those who had come from the LGBTQ community. The mic would be theirs. Something remarkable happened that night that changed both groups. The activists found genuine empathy and compassion from those they thought hated them, and the church members gathered were given a chance to show love to the outsiders who spoke out of their truth and past pain.[2]

> What is the place of wilderness in your life? Where might there be a door for grace to enter and make new what may have become stone in you?

Repair is something we can feel internally. It is when we don't get what we deserve or had hoped to receive. It is the undeserved pardon, a welcoming hand of forgiveness when we expected rebuke or to be turned away. It is the father running toward his broken and repentant son in the parable Jesus told his followers (Luke 15:11–32). In repair, we have the opportunity to forgive and run toward one another by bringing light into the darkness and reconciling what was designed to be together.

For Reflection and Discussion

1 Think of a relationship you have been in that needed repair. How did you resolve the disconnection? Did you use any of the NAME IT elements? If you didn't get to repair, can you imagine now what might have been helpful to make a shift?

2 Think of your current relationships. Is there one in particular that might need some repair work? How might the NAME IT steps be applied here? Have you tried any of them yet?

3 Take some time to journal an action plan for repairing this relationship. Think about what the setting would need to be, who should be there, and how might you imagine the conversation going. It is important you anticipate your own and the other person's blocks to being able to NAME IT together.

4 How is repair tied to redemption and God's purposes in your own life?

In repair, we have the opportunity to forgive and run toward one another by bringing light into the darkness and reconciling what was designed to be together.

4

Navigating Romantic Relationships

EVERYONE WANTS great relationships, but far too few of us actually accomplish the goal. What is getting in the way of spending more time basking in the light of connection? Why do so many of us settle for distance and protection? To answer these questions, we need to understand strategies that do and don't work as we attempt to navigate the challenges common in relationships.

John and Danielle are high-school sweethearts who find solace from the shortcomings and challenges of their families in each other's arms. Growing up, both felt invisible and unwanted. Together they discover what they always wanted: unconditional love and boundless attention. John and Danielle bring out the best in each other, and their fairly-tale romance provides real-life evidence for the prospect of soul mates. They thoroughly enjoy each other's company, and their relationship is fun, easy, and meaningful. Everyone who saw them on their wedding day could feel the intense power of their connection and tap into the universal longing for reciprocal adoration. John and Danielle seem destined for a lifetime of happiness and sharing in the delights of growing old together.

Unfortunately, soon after the honeymoon, John and Danielle come crashing down into the harsh reality of figuring out life together. The magical glow quickly dissipates, causing them to question whether love "till death do us part" is a genuine possibility. The daily drudgery of work and everyday life maintenance often creates distance and disconnection. The strong love between partners seems to get chipped away as the years mount. Complicating distance are

What is getting in the way of spending more time basking in the light of connection?

issues such as miscommunication, different viewpoints and styles, mistrust, addictions, abuse, affairs, and intimacy problems. There are so many stresses that constantly barrage our relationships, no wonder so many don't survive. People point to a divorce rate of 40 percent as proof that marriage is outdated, ineffective, and unnecessary. Why sign up for a serious long-term contract with just one person when you can be a free agent playing the field, enjoying the benefits of multiple people vying for your services?

We take a very different position. We are astounded that 60 percent of marriages last a lifetime despite the relentless challenges. Most married people do not have a clear image of what love is, what they are looking for in marriage, or what it takes to make a marriage work. Combine the lack of awareness with persistent stress and you would think the odds of making a marriage work are close to zero. Two very different people navigating a wild world with all the freedom to leave at any moment is a recipe for a breakup. Yet, more couples make it for a lifetime than do not. How is this possible? What powerful force is responsible for the odds being in favor of marriages lasting?

What Are We Really Looking For?

The ancient Greeks called love "the madness of the gods." Most of us can't really define what love is. We think of it as some mysterious, volatile mixture of romance and sentimentality that randomly waxes and wanes. There is no manual to explain what works. No wonder so many of us struggle in relationships. We need to get clear instructions on what love is and what we are looking for. What is the key to great relationships and marriages? Is it a friendship, a negotiation, a business deal, an exchange of skills, or an impossibility?

We have amazing news to share: the secret, mysterious code of what love is has finally been cracked. It is not so mysterious after all. We are a social species hardwired to connect, cooperate, and bond. Love is the answer to our basic, built-in need to belong and have a

What is the key to great relationships and marriages?

Love is the answer to our basic, built-in need to belong and have a safe place to connect to and a secure home from which to explore the world.

safe place to connect to and a secure home from which to explore the world. Love is much more than a mixed bag of feelings; it is an emotional bond with high degrees of engagement, vulnerability, and responsiveness. An emotional bond with a loved one is a potent source of resilience and provides the best antidote to stress. Our ability to reach out for calming and comfort to someone with whom we feel connected is our greatest strength. Knowing that we matter, that we are important and worth something to another person, is the universal longing of our hearts. Nothing can replace this yearning to share the load for mutual benefit. This emotional need to attach, to become part of something bigger than ourselves, is the basic instinct of humans, not survival of the fittest. To survive and thrive, we need to surround ourselves with others willing to make our needs as important as their own, just as we need to make their needs as important as our own.

Learning to pay attention to what is most essential, our emotional bond, helps couples to not get lost in all the noise of their relationship. Most couples falsely believe it is the specific content of an interaction or actions themselves that cause a fight. Maybe the focus is the critical comment about your weight or your partner checking Facebook instead of talking or the same old fight over where to spend the holidays. These issues trigger us very differently depending on the state of the relationship. If you want to go out with your friends and your relationship is in a good place, then it's probable your partner supports your decision to have fun. If your relationship is in a distressed place, then chances are high your partner is going to have a problem with you going out with your friends again. It's not about all the "noise" of going out with your friends, it's really about how safe the relationship is. Instead of wasting time trying to fix all the issues and figure out who is wrong or right, which often causes us to lose focus on the bond, we need to concentrate our attention on what is most important: the connection. Putting our energies toward seeking solutions to details that trigger fights often distracts our awareness from where we need it most: our longings to be seen, heard, understood, and cared about. Possessing a map of love that shows where the destination of connection is located makes it a lot easier for couples to navigate the landscape of love. Listening to our heart's GPS will tell us if we are off track (disconnected), recalculating (repairing), or arriving at our destination (connected).

The easiest way to assess the current state of our emotional bond is by measuring the quality of engagement between partners. Keeping it really simple: strongly bonded couples are focused on what is happening right now in their relationship. When we are engaged, we are interested, curious, alive, and actively participating. Couples with low engagement are distracted, busy, and distant. They pay poor attention. We all know how bad it feels when you are excited and want to share an experience with someone and you notice they are not really listening or, even worse, are looking over your shoulder to see if they can talk to someone more stimulating. Couples don't separate because their love fails; couples break up because the quality of engagement plummets.

Three Roads toward Connection

Typically, when couples meet the engagement is high. Remember your first date? Time slows down as you and your partner stare into each other's eyes and hang on each word. Often doing something they both like, couples find it easy to enjoy one another's company and have fun. If only couples could spend their whole relationship in this honeymoon period of enthusiastic participation.

There are three roads couples can take toward connection. The high, happy road is the fun stuff of relationships—going out to dinner, watching a movie, enjoying a vacation, or having sex. This is the good stuff of mutual responsiveness and the reason we get into relationships. We all want to spend as much time as possible traveling the high road of pleasure.

The middle road is the regular stuff of everyday life, the daily grind of work and the basic logistics we face waking up each morning—

Listening to our heart's GPS will tell us if we are off track (disconnected), recalculating (repairing), or arriving at our destination (connected).

paying bills, driving car pool, cleaning the house, doing laundry, and so forth. This middle road is practical and necessary for maintaining our lifestyles. The monotonous toil often introduces stress and distance to relationships. Most couples plan to spend more time on the high road, but the time-consuming middle leaves little time or energy for it. Planned date nights get harder and harder to execute over time when the to-do list is ever expanding.

The low, dark road is where we experience the bumps, bruises, and hurts of life. This is where couples share their struggles, fears, and vulnerabilities. Most couples try to avoid this road if at all possible. Inevitably, though, life throws us all challenges that trigger our insecurities and feelings of helplessness, rejection, and failure. The question is, What do we do with these vulnerable parts of ourselves? Sadly, it is in these places of fears, hurts, and insecurities, places where we need others the most, that we often find ourselves isolated in the coldness of disconnection.

The low road is the least travelled for most couples, because partners choose to walk it alone. To endure the discomfort of the low road alone, we all develop strategies to survive. The two most common defensive strategies are to use either anger or avoidance to hide our vulnerabilities. Yet, we pay a high price for our self-protection. The cost of hiding the inconvenient parts of ourselves is that there is less of us to engage and love.

It seems most relationships tend to follow a similar developmental path. Early on in the honeymoon phase, couples spend a lot of time on the high road, some on the middle road, and very little on the low road. Most of us hold this ideal as a template for the best relationships. Our favorite fairy tales end with eternal love on the high road and living "happily ever after." As relationships mature and couples face the challenges of everyday life, time spent on the high road reduces as the need to walk the middle road takes over. In this phase, couples try to avoid the low road of fears and discomfort because they already are experiencing less of the happiness of the high road, and they don't want to lose anymore.

The decisions couples make in this intermediate period of their lives are critical. The grind of the middle road exhausts our resources and makes engagement more difficult. Inevitably, the prolonged middle road creates distance in relationships. Increased distance usually equates to increased defensiveness, mistrust, and need for additional protection. As both partners' defenses strengthen their fears, insecurities and vulnerabilities are bound to rise. The simple choice is what to do with the rising vulnerabilities? Do couples allow the stress of the middle road to force them to walk the low road together, or do they face their fears apart? Sadly, most couples don't realize the huge opportunity for connection on the low road, and their lack of awareness and choice to not share inevitably leads to further distress and isolation.

We believe the best blueprint for strong, vibrant, and flexible relationships is to share the high, middle, and low roads together. It is a foolish and dangerous goal to believe your relationship can perpetually stay on the high road and avoid the low road. If you can join your partner wherever they are, then the math is in your favor to achieve the highest levels of engagement. Meeting your partner on a romantic date (high road), paying bills together (middle road), or sharing the trials of a long day (low road) gives couples the most options for finding connection anywhere life takes them.

What Happens When We Don't Get What We Need

While connection is the destination of all three roads, the distance and distress of disconnection is the predictable byproduct of failing to walk together. We do better when those we trust are by our sides, especially in times of struggle on the low road. When people let us down in moments of need, we have only a limited number of ways to protect ourselves. There are two general options for action when connection fails—move toward or move away from the source of disconnection. We all do some of both, but we tend to default to the move that worked best early in life. As the "still face" experiment in chapter 2 suggests, how parents respond to their children heavily shapes how children learn to interact in the world, learning they

The best blueprint for strong, vibrant, and flexible relationships is to share the high, middle, and low roads together.

How parents respond to their children heavily shapes how children learn to interact in the world, learning they carry into adulthood.

carry into adulthood. The different parent/child interactions in the "still face" experiment can be organized into four general styles of connecting to others: secure, anxious, avoidant, or disorganized.

Securely connected (also called "attached" in psychology literature) children trust in their parents' responsiveness to their needs, and therefore they are the most direct in turning toward their parents for comfort. Because they feel safe, they also find it the easiest to move away from their parents to explore the world. This ability to freely move depending on their changing needs is the hallmark of secure attachment. For the most part, the child expects both moving toward and away to work well. Picture a little boy running too fast and falling in the playground, skinning his knee. A securely connected child runs to get a hug and a Band-Aid, then runs back to play with his friends.

Anxiously connected children find it difficult to move *away from* others. They constantly cling for reassurance as they seek relief for their anxiety. Inconsistent, anxious parenting makes it difficult for anxious children to trust the comfort will be available. Unlike the securely connected child who expects good things in moving toward, anxiously connected kids do not seem to get enough of the comfort they need, leaving them with a feeling of scarcity not abundance. Going back to our example of the playground, the anxiously connected child is reluctant to explore on his own, because he is afraid of something bad happening. He stays close to his parents.

Avoidantly connected kids find it difficult to move *toward* others. Overbearing, controlling, and distant parenting produces avoidant kids who learn to self-soothe rather than to seek comfort. If no one is going to respond, then you get good at taking care of yourself and not needing others. This ability to take care of yourself is adaptive and necessary for healthy development when done in moderation. However, if the turning away toward independence is persistent, then the cost is to sacrifice the ability to share vulnerability. Never letting people in to comfort our fears and insecurities sets us up to not know how to connect on the low road and guaranteeing we face fear in isolation. Back to the playground, the avoidantly attached kid skins his knee and quickly wipes away his tears on his own.

Disorganized attached children have trouble *both* moving toward and away from others. A parent who is supposed to be a source of safety but instead is abusive creates kids who get stuck in the anxiety of needing support yet not feeling safe enough to seek the comfort they need. They swing back and forth between needing support and pushing it away. Although these mixed signals may appear crazy, they make absolute sense when you understand their predicament of feeling unsafe. Back to the playground, a disorganized attached boy skins his knee and walks backward toward his parent. He is stuck in the anxiety of needing comfort and knowing it is likely he will get in trouble. This conflicted state leads to sending mixed, confusing signals, which only exacerbates the lack of safety.

Although these connection styles can be modified in adulthood, they heavily influence how each of us reacts to our needs and how we go about getting our needs met. No wonder so many of our current adult relationships often feel so eerily similar to childhood relationships. Recognizing our connection style is important in helping us understand the good reasons we make the moves that we do. These consistent moves toward or away are ways we attempt to protect ourselves. Knowing our moves is the first step to figuring out how they impact our partner and their moves.

At times, all couples get stuck in protective, reactive conversations where each partner's protective moves feed the other's protective moves. Like a familiar dance, cycles of disconnection generally follow the same steps. Both partners get caught doing what works for them but not their partner. To understand these negative patterns, we need to look past the triggers, details, and logistics of what they are fighting about and pay attention to the moves.

Recognizing our connection style is important in helping us understand the good reasons we make the moves that we do.

Two Worlds Collide

Let's take a look at an interaction between John and Danielle, the honeymoon couple we introduced at the start of this chapter, to help shed light on these predictable patterns of disconnection. We'll fast forward ten years. They now have three children, and the time they spend together on the high road of connection is dwindling as the years pass. They are grinding away on the middle road, and they don't do the low road together. Danielle has an anxious attachment style and pushes for comfort for her anxiety, while John has an avoidant style that tries to reduce anxiety by moving away. Here is an exchange they had last week.

Like most of us, the couple wakes in the morning tired from a lack of sleep and the demands of the previous day. They are polite to each other as they get ready for work and send the kids off to school. Each with a cup of coffee in hand, they give each other a kiss goodbye and head off in separate directions. At work, Danielle starts thinking about their relationship and the distance creeping in. Her worries prompt her to reach out to John for some reassurance, so she decides to write a text:

> Hey, John, just touching base. I wanted to find some time to talk today. Nothing big, just hoping we can connect. Hope all is good with you. Thanks for working so hard.

John is swamped at work when he receives Danielle's text. He is hoping everything is okay and there isn't a problem that maybe he doesn't know about. Although, he doesn't have time to talk, he also knows if he doesn't respond, it usually leads to a fight, so he replies:

>

Danielle receives his text and is immediately frustrated. She reached out to connect and directly express her need to talk, and John can't even find two minutes for a quick call or even a few sentences. Her dissatisfaction is expressed in an angry text back:

> Are you kidding me? I asked to talk and you send a smiley face, really? I'm stressed out worrying about our relationship and you couldn't care less. I certainly would make some time if you needed me. This is so unfair. Why is work more important than me?

When John's text alert sounds so quickly after he sent the smiley face, his gut lets him know there is a problem. During a meeting at work, he looks down to scan the sentences. Sure enough, Danielle is unhappy with him, just what he feared. How the heck is he supposed to explain why work is more important than her? There is no point talking about this now, so John decides to put if off until he gets home and puts the cellphone away in his pocket without replying.

Despite her duties at work, Danielle keeps checking her phone for John's response. Her anger brews as the minutes turn to hours of silence. She tries to distract herself with work, but the pull of the phone keeps bringing her back to check. Every time she checks, she gets mad at John and mad at herself for being so needy. She wants to stop checking her phone, thinking, if he is not going to put in an effort for their relationship, then why should she? But the anxiety keeps overriding her willpower. After feeling the hurt of rejection every time she checks the phone and weighing her many options, Danielle decides to disregard the texting and go old school with a phone call to John.

John is good at compartmentalizing, which helps him focus on the task at hand and block out distractions, such as worrying about his relationship while he is at work. When his phone rings with Danielle's number, his stomach drops. He knows Danielle is upset, and the inevitable, dreaded fight is coming for him. Not wanting any scenes at work, John shakes his head and chooses to not answer his phone, wanting to deal with the issue at home after work.

When John doesn't answer his phone, especially at a time of day when he is usually available, Danielle is livid. His decision to intentionally leave her "hanging" in her time of distress is outrageous and unacceptable. If she accepts this treatment, that bodes poorly for the future. Filled with righteous anger, she jumps into her car and drives to his office. Overwhelmed with emotion, any response, even a fight, is a better option for Danielle than silence.

John is working at his desk when there is a knock at the door. He says, "Come in" and is surprised to see Danielle heatedly stride into his office. Trying to calm the situation, he says, "I'm sorry, it's been a crazy day and my phone is giving me problems. I'm really looking forward to talking tonight." For a brief moment, John actually wishes he had dropped his phone in the toilet. Sometimes the cost of a new phone is worth the price for a good, believable excuse. Danielle is past the point of reason and blasts away, "You weren't planning on talking tonight, so stop lying. You don't care about anyone but yourself. I'm not going to put up with this anymore. I deserve better than this, someone who works as hard in this relationship as me. You need to work harder at communicating, or I'm not sure I can do this anymore."

Not able to stop the escalation, John uses anger to try to get Danielle to back off. He says, "I can't help it you need to talk so much. Maybe you need to talk to a therapist and work on your issues. I'm not sure I can keep dealing with this drama anymore either. Please leave before you make a scene." Danielle with tears in her eyes storms out of his office. Dejected, John lays his head down on his desk and sighs in exasperation.

Look at how quickly a simple, harmless reaching-out text can intensify into threats of separation. To understand each partner's moves in this fight, we need to explore the two very different ways they handle the stress of disconnection. Danielle was looking for comfort for her anxiety, while John was hoping to avoid a fight. Neither got what they were hoping for.

Understanding the World of Withdrawers

Withdrawers learn at an early age that the best way for them to handle their pain is to try to avoid it. Making our vulnerable needs invisible is necessary when no one is offering comfort. The root of withdrawal is a failure of others to respond in times of need. To survive, withdrawers learn to do it alone. If no one meets them on their low road, in their fears and suffering, the only plausible path forward is for withdrawers to do what they can to escape the pain. Experiencing the intense agony of suffering in isolation, they make a decision to not feel and do what they can to avoid feeling that way again. Picture a baby crying hysterically and a parent never responding; the baby learns to stop crying.

Withdrawers, like John, truly believe the best way to protect themselves and their relationship during stressful times is to pull away to diffuse the situation. They are looking to self-soothe and handle the stress on their own and not look for help. This independence works well in many areas of their lives. Turning off their feelings and cognitively focusing on the task at hand helps withdrawers to perform well under pressure. No matter the career—soldier, police officer, doctor, lawyer, business owner, or teacher—our culture expects and encourages staying calm in the face of challenges.

Withdrawers are good at deactivating their alarm signals to get the job done well. This real-life training to handle stress well by shutting off feelings is hugely beneficial and well rewarded in our society. For many withdrawers, "getting the job done" is how they find success, get promoted, fit in, and feel good about themselves. Measuring their own performance is often a barometer for how safe and needed they feel. A good performance equates to acceptance, while a bad performance leads to rejection and isolation. With all their energies focused on what they need to do to succeed and fix things, there is little left over to pay attention to their inner, vulnerable experience. When describing their feelings, they often use general, vague words. They say they feel numb or nothing at all, that they

Withdrawers learn at an early age that the best way for them to handle their pain is to try to avoid it. Making our vulnerable needs invisible is necessary when no one is offering comfort.

Withdrawers are good at deactivating their alarm signals to get the job done well.

Being self-reliant leaves little room for healthy dependency and communicating vulnerability.

Withdrawers are vigilant to dodge fighting and messages that they are doing it wrong, rather than seeking the good stuff of relationship—comfort and connection.

feel confused or don't know what they feel, or that they do not understand the question.

Unfortunately, this avoidance strategy around vulnerability that originally helped as a child to deal with a lack of comfort and that gets reinforced at work comes at a huge price in adult relationships. Being self-reliant leaves little room for healthy dependency and communicating vulnerability. The walls they put up to keep negative emotions from getting in the way also prevent them from repairing and joining their partner on the low road. It is impossible to emotionally engage in vulnerability when your body trusts in moving away. To make matter worse, these indiscriminate walls designed to keep out the negative also keep out the positive emotions. To protect ourselves from anger and yelling, the walls we erect also snuff out the laughter and love. How ironic that the attempt to avoid the low road also reduces the ability to go on the high road. Maybe this partly explains why baby boys (with small walls) smile on average 350 times a day while old men (big walls) only smile on average 3 times a day.

Given the withdrawer's focus on avoiding the negative, we can see the appeal of creating walls and moving away. Withdrawers are vigilant to dodge fighting and messages that they are doing it wrong, rather than seeking the good stuff of relationship—comfort and connection. The rule they unquestioningly follow is to avoid the low road at all costs because it rarely ends well for them. Why would they want to have a conversation around their partner's struggle when to truly empathize with their partner's emotions, they would have to feel their own emotions? Empathy is "feeling with" others, and withdrawers learned early on that the best way to deal with their pain and fears is to avoid feeling. So, they are set up to fail at empathizing with their partner.

Tragically, distancing themselves from feelings and not listening to their emotional signals only guarantees they will not know who they are and what they need emotionally. The failure to receive responsiveness to their vulnerable needs sets them up to not know how to ask for help and to also not know how to respond vulnerably to their partner. It is a pretty unfair arrangement that withdrawers are taught to shut down and then are celebrated in their jobs for turning off emotions only to find in their relationships they are blamed for not knowing how to come forward emotionally. Their partners, frustrated at being left alone, tell the withdrawers there is something wrong with them, that they are emotionally crippled, and they dejectedly believe it. How are they supposed to know how to respond to vulnerability when no one responded to their vulnerability? In avoiding their emotions, withdrawers remain alone in their need and are also set up to not know how to respond to their partner's needs.

What is so beautiful is that withdrawers keep trying to respond to their partner's vulnerable needs even though they rarely receive it themselves. That is the power of love. No matter how emotionally depriving our experiences, nothing can extinguish our longing to be in connection.

As therapists, we work with many withdrawers like Hector, a marine sergeant who grew up in an abusive family where he was totally on his own. To cope, he turned to alcohol and video games. His ability to emotionally shut down worked well in his profession and was reinforced with many promotions and accolades. His relationship history was a train wreck of constant fighting and infidelity. Then he met Maria, and something inside him shifted. Although he always avoided doing vulnerability, something deep in his heart craved to be there for Maria. Imagine how scary it is to go down to the low road when you have never done it before. Hector's courage to take the low road and give Maria what he never received is an inspiring testimony to how love grows us.

The way withdrawers learn to come forward instead of moving away in relationships is for them to experience the power of vulnerability. Instead of avoiding the negatives, they come to see the opportunity in their struggles. As therapists, we invite withdrawers to face their inner demons and share them with their partner. If the

In avoiding their emotions, withdrawers remain alone in their need and are also set up to not know how to respond to their partner's needs.

The way withdrawers learn to come forward instead of moving away in relationships is for them to experience the power of vulnerability.

Withdrawers who can both turn off their feelings to handle pressure situations and make friends with their inner world to vulnerably reach to their partner have the highest degrees of engagement and the most pathways to connection.

Pursuers believe the best way to protect themselves and their relationship during stressful times is to push their partner to respond.

root cause of withdrawal is a failure of others to respond, then the healing solution is found in the arms of another. It is always easy to love someone who is on top of the world, but when they really need love is at the bottom. When withdrawers are loved in their failures and broken places, they can finally appreciate the true power of connection. We are not designed to do well alone on the low road. Receiving love, especially in our moments of darkness, makes it a lot easier to appreciate its value and to return the gift to one's partner.

In the end, we are not trying to turn withdrawers into pursuers. Rather, we are trying to expand withdrawers' range of behaviors, so they can walk all three roads of connection. Withdrawers who can both turn off their feelings to handle pressure situations and make friends with their inner world to vulnerably reach to their partner have the highest degrees of engagement and the most pathways to connection.

Understanding the World of Pursuers

Pursuers believe the best way to protect themselves and their relationship during stressful times is to push their partner to respond. Like the root of withdrawal, the root of pursuing is a failure of others to respond in times of need. Anxiety is a signal asking for help, and when the assistance doesn't come, then you either keep asking or give up. We are designed to look for help with our anxiety, so we can face the threat together. This overt longing "to be in relationship" to face challenges certainly has many advantages. Pursuers tend to be better at talking, expressing their feelings, and communicating their needs. Spending more time paying attention to the relationship, they usually are quicker to notice problems and more motivated to bridge distance.

In general, pursuers are more comfortable being dependent and a part of a team. They want to do whatever is necessary to make the relationship work, and if that means staying up all night talking and trying to repair after a fight, then so be it. This energy to confront relationship issues is a real strength when the push elicits movement in the right direction. As therapists, we often find it is the pursuer who makes the first phone call, who talks the most in therapy, who actually does the homework assignments, and who wants to stay in treatment.

The pushing makes sense, but when you understand the world of withdrawers it is easy to see how the pushing doesn't bring the withdrawers closer, as hoped, but rather makes the withdrawers go further away. Withdrawers don't want to stay up all night talking; they'd rather go to bed. Left alone to manage the stress, pursuers spin their wheels and often cannot find relief for their anxiety. When the people we love stop fighting for the relationship, stop investing in it, and stop paying attention to what is happening, then the distance starts to stealthily take over.

Pursuers often describe feeling hurt, alone, not wanted, invisible, sad, deprived, unheard, disconnected, unimportant, and desperate. To manage the rollercoaster of emotions, pursuers seek help wherever they can find it—friends, self-help books, Dr. Phil, therapists, or prayer. They are motivated to work hard in the relationship. Pursuers are not even looking for a 50/50 effort from their partner; they are willing to do more. They just want their partner to engage and make some effort.

When withdrawers fail to engage despite the pursuers' push to do so, then the pursuers are left with two options for handling the isolation—be enraged at the unfairness of being left alone, or feel horrible about themselves for being rejected. Which one would you choose? It makes sense that so many pursuers are good at being angry and critical. They are trying to create change and motivate their partner to do something differently. If they can get their partner to listen and follow their advice, then things can improve.

The alternative, to not push, doesn't seem plausible, because they believe if they do not say anything to their partner, then chances are high that nothing will change. Often the pursuer's hope for change is embedded in their critical messages. Anger is their way of

It makes sense that so many pursuers are good at being angry and critical. They are trying to create change and motivate their partner to do something differently.

The pursuers' vigilance and relentless energy are intended to provide protection from rejection.

signaling that something is wrong, and the anger provides energy to move forward and fix the problem. When you understand the function of their anger, it is easy to realize why fighting is a much better option than silence. Silence breaks the interpersonal bridge and plummets the pursuer into the depths of suffering and separation.

The pursuers' vigilance and relentless energy are intended to provide protection from rejection. Yet when they feel abandoned, it is hard for them to not doubt their own value and lovability. Think back to moments when you were not picked to play on a team or were left out by a certain click of friends or maybe by that someone you had a crush on. How do we make sense of such rebuffs? Most of us conclude there is something wrong with us. Despite our best attempts—practicing hard, getting a new outfit, working out, or putting on makeup—we are still not chosen.

It is anguishing to want to fit in only to find ourselves on the outside. As if the pain, sadness, and isolation weren't enough, pursuers often find that in this moment of utter desperation, when they are cut off from others, they also turn on themselves. They turn that same anger inward that they use to motivate their partner, because there is no partner to focus the anger on. Pursuers beat themselves up by saying things like, "I deserve it, I'm a loser, I'm stupid, I'm ugly, I'm a fake, I knew this is where I would end up." Tragically, pursuers learn to hide this self-talk because they don't want their fears confirmed. The toxic environment—externally criticizing your partner while internally criticizing yourself and hiding your vulnerabilities—makes it almost impossible to feel safe and connected.

The constant vacillation between the protest and anger in relationship and the sadness and fear of disconnection is crazy-making for pursuers.

The constant vacillation between the protest and anger in relationship and the sadness and fear of disconnection is crazy-making for pursuers. They work so hard to feel confident and upbeat, yet the persistent reproof of their partner's withdrawal brings out the worst in pursuers. Many pursuers feel they are set up to become monsters. They know they are often too critical and negative, but the alternative of being alone is a worse option than fighting and nagging.

Anyone spending so much time stuck between anger and rejection is going to be anxious. It is pretty sad that pursuers are then blamed for being so insecure. It is certainly unfair that the fear of rejection, a natural byproduct of experiencing real rejection, is then used as evidence that there is something wrong with the pursuer, and heartbreakingly, the pursuer also believes this anxiety is proof there is something broken inside them.

We need to help pursuers realize their anxiety and anger are natural responses to surviving the pain of disconnection. Validating their self-protection creates the safety to find another way of getting their needs met. Instead of coming forward with a weapon, we as therapists want to help them come forward in a softer way to seek comfort and not assign blame. The only way to do this is to help pursuers plug into their underlying vulnerabilities and share them with their partner.

This is risky stuff, because if someone shares their greatest fear that deep down inside they feel broken and unlovable and their partner agrees they are unlovable, then the ultimate rejection feels like a death sentence. Yet, if the pursuers never ask for what they need, then they're also guaranteed to never receive the comfort they so desperately need in these dreadfully dark places. We invite pursuers to embrace the low road and invite their partner into it, too. Ultimately the cure for rejection is love and acceptance in our damaged places.

> Ultimately the cure for rejection is love and acceptance in our damaged places.

Good News

If pursuers are from the hot planet of Venus and withdrawers are from the cold planet of Mars, it seems any relationship between the two is fundamentally ill-matched and destined for misery. Although this conclusion may seem logical, it is flawed because it doesn't account for the amazing opportunity for growth when two

It seems God has planted into our hearts an attraction to someone different than ourselves.

opposite forces learn to synchronize. Blending two very different truths creates a much larger whole than bringing together two similar truths. It seems God has planted into our hearts an attraction to someone different than ourselves. Certainly, two people who are very alike have a better chance of getting along, but their potential to help each other grow is severely limited. Two dissimilar people are going to find it more difficult to coordinate their moves, but if they can get into sync, then their potential for growth is more expansive. No wonder the traits that drive you nuts about your partner are also the ones that hold so much promise for your own transformation.

For example, if your partner's messiness has frustrated you for years and your partner has resisted all your attempts to "fix" it, then perhaps there is a lesson in this constant bickering. Maybe the neat partner needs to "loosen up" a little bit to round out his sharp edges. Maybe the "sloppy" partner needs to develop a bit of order and "tighten up" her nonchalant approach. If they listen to each other's important messages, then their different styles provide precisely the balance needed. What a great system when it works. And when it doesn't, it provides opportunities to connect on the low road.

When we look at how pursuers and withdrawers interact, both partners believe that the other has more choice in making their moves than they actually do. It's easy for a pursuer to think, "Why does my partner walk away when talking is so much better?" A withdrawer can easily think, "Why does my partner choose to push and fight when walking away is so much better?" What both fail to realize is these moves are strongly ingrained, stemming all the way back to their childhoods. These defensive moves helped each to survive in earlier relationships, and it is likely that if both partners exit their current relationship, their moves are going to be similar in the next.

Many of our emotional decisions run on automaticity, the ability to do things without consciously thinking about them. When we practice something long enough, we develop a muscle memory that performs the action without our needing to think about it. An example of automaticity is driving: most of us think about everything else but the actual driving itself.

Looking at the neurological function of the brain, we notice that paying attention to all the details takes a tremendous amount of energy (glucose) to run, so it is efficient for many of our actions to run outside of our awareness. The downside is that when much of our emotional life functions on autopilot, we make spontaneous moves that seem to protect us in the short-term without seeing the costs of those moves on our partner and our relationship in the long-run. Couples who learn to slow down their process and consciously face the present situation are empowered to finally make a choice about their emotional responses.

The next challenge after shifting out of automaticity is trying to discover new ways to engage. If both partners are conscious at the critical moments of a fight, they will realize that they both face bad choices. The pursuer's questions are, "Do I push my partner to talk, which gives me hope for change but makes him feel uncomfortable and pull away, leaving me alone? Or do I say nothing, which stops the fight but leaves me alone with my fears and hurt?" No matter which course the pursuer chooses, they end up alone. The withdrawers face similar no-win questions. "Do I go away to avoid the fight, which makes me feel safe but leaves my partner feeling abandoned? Or do I try to stay and absorb the pain and the message that I'm failing?" Recognizing that the one thing you do to protect yourself also devastates your partner creates a real dilemma. What option do you usually choose?

The wonderful news is there is another option. Instead of settling for survival and self-protection, we can discover growth and healing. The secret is in directly revealing our vulnerable needs, which we have camouflaged underneath our protective strategies. The way out of the negative cycle is responsiveness, not additional protection. Partners need to shift their communication away from defensiveness and justification and toward openness and reciprocity. Both partners

Many of our emotional decisions run on automaticity, the ability to do things without consciously thinking about them. An example of automaticity is driving: most of us think about everything else but the actual driving itself.

Instead of settling for survival and self-protection, we can discover growth and healing.

need to recognize that the moment of their fight is really their moment of greatest need.

Choosing self-protection guarantees a "mutual miss," where each partner is not responding with comfort but instead is actually doing the worst thing possible for their partner's well-being. Accepting responsibility for the impact our move has on our partner starts a new process of working together instead of against each other. Withdrawers need to acknowledge they are experts at the move most devastating to their pursuer partner: walking away. Pursuers must admit that they are masters at the most debilitating move for their withdrawer partner: confrontation and criticism.

Every partner faces the same choice: remain part of the problem or become part of the solution. The person who is exceptional at responding to their partner in the worst way possible can change their moves and become the source of healing and safety. Talk about an exciting turnaround or miracle! Instead of taking the bait and reinforcing each other's defensive moves, which continue to conceal both partner's vulnerable needs, we are advocating that partners unite to create a positive cycle of responsiveness. If we focus on the vicious moment where the couple is perfectly missing each other in a fight, we can see the possibilities for a different outcome. Underneath the pursuer's screaming is a partner terrified of abandonment, and behind the withdrawer's walls is a partner scared of criticism. Both share the same truth: their underlying need for comfort in their fears goes unseen and unmet by their partner. Both deserve reassurance and love in their places of doubt and darkness, but they don't know how to ask for it directly.

To achieve a lasting, resilient, loving bond, we must be able to tune into our deeper vulnerable needs and communicate them into clear signals, so our partner can respond. Instead of self-protection, which pushes our partner away, we offer emotional honesty and openness, which pulls our partner closer.

> To achieve a lasting, resilient, loving bond, we must be able to tune into our deeper vulnerable needs and communicate them into clear signals, so our partner can respond.

Let's take a look at John and Danielle, our texting-fight couple, to see how couples can repair a fight and create a vulnerable conversation that creates safety and security for both.

NAME IT

After their fight at his office, John is driving home on autopilot toward what he believes will be another inevitable fight when he opens the front door. Determined to get better results, John begins the NAME IT process by Noticing and reflecting on how he feels about his relationship. He desperately wants peace and happiness, and yet he keeps finding fighting and frustration. Noticing the pressure that he feels in his shoulders and chest, John admits to himself his feelings of being trapped and helpless, with no good options. No part of him wants to talk about this when he gets home, because he already knows the outcome—more fighting and distance. Retreating seems a better option to avoid escalation, and yet John clearly understands there is no way Danielle is not going to talk about this when he walks in.

As John allows his feelings of helplessness and reluctance to talk emerge, he begins to engage with his own experience instead of avoiding it. Listening more deeply to his emotional signals, John starts to notice how uncomfortable he is with fighting and hearing about what he is doing wrong. Confrontation makes him feel like a loser, and if he keeps on this course of letting Danielle down, he fears eventually she'll move on, leaving him alone and breaking up their family.

John never talks about these fears, hurts, and insecurities, because he believes the best way to handle these feelings is to endure them alone and wait for them to pass. This time, as John listens to his vulnerable feelings, they start to point him to move in toward Danielle instead of his typical response, going away. What John's heart needs is comfort and reassurance in his fears, not avoidance. As he thinks about the possibility of sharing what he is feeling, John imagines his son feeling the same fears as he does and how much

John would want to comfort his son and not leave him alone in his pain. Is it possible he deserves the same comfort and companionship as his son?

Armed with new information about his underlying vulnerable truth, John possesses the necessary starting materials for a different conversation with Danielle. Understanding more clearly the function of his withdrawal to protect himself from confrontation but also the costs of hiding his heart, John is open to exploring and Acknowledging Danielle's moves. Hopeful for a different outcome, John opens the door and says to Danielle, "Hey, I've been thinking a lot about us, and I really want to talk about ways we can communicate differently. We are both frustrated with what happened, and although I think I figured out some of what is bothering me, I want to know more about what is bothering you and your version of what went down."

John's approach is open and non-blaming. He understands his defensive moves and wants to know more about Danielle's so they can change their dance together. John's plan is to ask Danielle the same questions he asked himself: "What does she feel when we fight, what does she do, and what does she really want?"

Danielle says, "I'm so tired of trying to get closer to you and you not showing up for me. I want to shake you when you don't respond. It drives me nuts."

John responds with curiosity, "I want to make sure I'm getting this right. When I don't respond you believe I don't care [what she feels], and you believe shaking me will get my attention [what she does]. It is hard for me to relate because I do the opposite; I head away from confrontation. I try to make myself smaller to avoid escalation. But I hear what you are saying; you want to get my attention."
John is confused, but trying to figure out her moves, he says, "So what you really want is to get closer to me with all those questions, comments, and requests [what she wants]? Okay, tell me more."
Asking your partner to "tell you more" is a great sentence that

demonstrates openness and curiosity. (Readers, feel free to borrow this line).

Danielle, with a pleading voice says, "Yes, I'm trying to connect, and when you walk away I feel so rejected, like you don't want to be around me." Starting to cry as she drops into her vulnerability, Danielle shares with a shaky voice, "I'm so alone and scared that maybe you are fed up with my nagging and want out of this relationship."

As the couple shifts the level of communication away from the specific details and toward their vulnerable feelings, they begin to see things in a new light. John responds empathetically, "Wow, I had no idea you felt scared. I just saw your anger and figured I screwed up again. I don't want to talk, because I believe it will only make things worse. Now I'm starting to see even though I hope walking away will calm things down, it actually makes you angrier."

As John starts to hold both truths and put their moves together (Merge), their negative cycle of Danielle pushing, triggering John's retreat, and John's withdrawal, triggering Danielle's pushing, plainly emerges. It is a chicken-or-egg debate, and both sides lose when automaticity takes over. As both partners accept responsibility for their steps in the negative dance, the couple initiates a radical shift by identifying the problems in their relationship. Instead of blaming each other, they begin to recognize that despite the different moves, they are both feeling the same feelings of loneliness, hurt, and fear underneath the self-protection. For good reasons, they are both guilty of not responding to each other's vulnerable needs. For the first time, united against their negative cycle, John and Danielle have a real shot at a successful repair.

To truly repair, we need to do more than identify what isn't working. More importantly, we must replace it with something better. As John and Danielle start to make sense of how they were set up to miss each other with their defenses, they create more safety for a new conversation based on their longings in their vulnerability. John, responding to Danielle's tears, says, "I'm so sorry

> To truly repair, we need to do more than identify what isn't working. More importantly, we must replace it with something better.

I didn't know how lonely you feel. I thought you'd rather be alone like I want to be." Reaching over he gives Danielle a hug and says, "Now that I know you get so scared, I'll just figure out how to stick around. I love you, and I want to be there for you in these tough spots. Thanks for letting me in." Danielle sinks into John's hug, relaxing her shoulders and whispering, "I love you too." Danielle and John connecting in their vulnerability (Embrace) is the ultimate goal of the NAME IT process. For the repair to be complete, both partners need someone to respond in their vulnerability. After their breakthrough, John and Danielle have a great night together. Their low-road conversation leads to a high road of smiles and laughter.

The following night, Danielle attempts to finish the repair process. After an enjoyable dinner, Danielle says, "I really appreciate you hanging in there with all my emotions last night. That felt great to feel you understanding my world better, and I want a chance to return the favor. I don't want to overwhelm you with questions, and it's ok if you are not ready to talk about it, but I am curious. What is it like for you when you are withdrawing?"

John responds, "Well, I feel pretty helpless, and I don't like it that I'm failing." Looking down at the floor with disappointment in his eyes, he says quietly, "It's ironic, because I feel similar to you, that if I keep failing you, maybe you'll leave me." Danielle immediately reaches over to give John a big kiss and hug, saying, "I'm sorry you are scared too, but I'm relieved you told me, and now I can make sure to let you know how proud I am of you. Even when you do get it wrong, it doesn't change my love for you."

With a wide grin John laughs and replies, "I never knew failing could feel so good. Maybe now that we are on a roll it is a good time to repair other past fights. Remember ten years ago at your mom's house we argued about—" With a mischievous smile, Danielle interrupts John by putting her finger over his lips and pulls him close for a passionate kiss.

This positive cycle of responsiveness is radically different from their negative cycle of defensiveness. The moment the vulnerable need

> For the repair to be complete, both partners need someone to respond in their vulnerability.

is met by your partner's loving response is the instant when the disconnection of the fight is transformed into the connection of repair. Instead of rejection, Danielle is rescued in her insecurities. Instead of feeling like a failure, John is accepted, especially when he gets it wrong. In their moments of greatest need, both partners actively respond with a definite yes.

It is imperative that couples don't simply settle for enjoying the newfound closeness after their Embrace moment. They need to Integrate the new experience into their existing relationship. It is possible, when partners know how to handle the ups and downs, for relationships to be much more stable and predictable than a perplexing, unnerving roller-coaster ride. Integrating the new moves of vulnerability into everyday life starts to replace the negative automaticity with positive automaticity. With practice, it is just as easy to create responsiveness memory as it is to be defensive. After their breakthrough bonding moment, John and Danielle commit to putting aside one hour a week to practice emotionally checking in with each other and having a vulnerable conversation. There are no shortcuts to learning a new language. Repetition is crucial to mastery.

To tie a bow on the NAME IT repair process, John and Danielle thank each other for the risks and responsiveness necessary to make it happen. Neither can replace a negative cycle on their own. It takes the integration of two truths to create a larger whole. In a funny twist, as the couple is falling asleep, John turns to Danielle and says, "Thank you for pushing me. I actually think I might like this vulnerability stuff." Laughing, Danielle replies, "Great! Can you try it on our kids and get them to go to bed? I'm going to try some of your withdrawal moves by going to sleep. See you in the morning, my love." As Danielle rolls over to get more comfortable, her laugh takes on an earnest tone and she says, "Thank you. This certainly is an amazing day, one I'll remember forever."

The moment the vulnerable need is met by your partner's loving response is the instant when the disconnection of the fight is transformed into the connection of repair.

Let's Not Forget about Sex

A chapter on romantic relationships is certainly incomplete without any mention of sex. Many people avoid talking about sex because it makes us feel uncomfortable. Yet, as we discussed previously, avoidance usually gets us in trouble. Lacking a clear target of what healthy sex looks like leaves us shooting blind in the dark. Refusing to engage in conversations about physical intimacy prevents us from turning on the lights. So, let's talk about sex.

Sex is simply a natural expression of an intimate, loving connection. Two people literally becoming one flesh, bonding together to fulfill a mutual longing to be seen and cherished. Sex is such a vulnerable act because in our nakedness we are open to experiencing the highs of desire and acceptance and the lows of failure and rejection. With such a wide range of potential outcomes, no wonder there is so much confusion out there as to what constitutes "great sex." Is it just a mysterious, incalculable mixture of sentiment, passion, compatibility, and lust?

How we define great sex is important. Our expectations often shape our reality. If we believe sex is merely a physical act focusing on an orgasm, then we are set up for sexual difficulties. Our culture's overemphasis on physiology, sexual mechanics, and performance unfortunately ignores the best part: the emotional and spiritual bond. Whenever the physical is disconnected from the emotional, then sex loses its luster and replaces the glory of communion with the selfishness of hedonism.

The exciting news is if we possess a clear understanding of what great sex is then there is something to celebrate that is much better than casual sex or boring, going-through-the-motions sex. We want to offer you a healthy, holistic definition of great sex. New sex research from cultures around the world shows that great sex is based on meaningful connection. Notice these universal findings. Great sex involves: (1) being present in the moment, (2) feeling in sync, (3) deep intimacy, (4) good communication and heightened

> How we define great sex is important. Our expectations often shape our reality.

> New sex research from cultures around the world shows that great sex is based on meaningful connection.

empathy, (5) authenticity, (6) exploration, (7) vulnerability, and (8) a sense of transcendence.[1] All these components emphasize God's design for sex to be a bonding event, not merely two separate muscles in spasm together. Disconnecting sex from its emotional and spiritual groundings is a formula for shallow intimacy.

Ultimately, we believe to restore a healthy perspective on sexuality, we must accentuate the benefits of the complete sexual package, including the physical, mental, emotional, and spiritual. It is tragic that so many people experience only limited, unfulfilling sexual encounters based on physical sensations. This cheap sex is like choosing to live on stale junk food instead of a delicious, nutritious, healthy, home-cooked meal. Let's expand our definition of great sex to include God's plan for true union and mutual adoration. In the magic of connection, there is no worry about the past or future, only the aliveness of the immediate moment to encounter ourselves, our partner, and God. Wherever we find love, God is always present.[2]

Spiritual Implications for Relationships

God has wired us for connection and has given us a longing in our hearts and souls to be known and to know others. He wants our full engagement to live in a way that connects us to God and to one another. The deeper meaning of religion isn't to help us earn a spot in heaven when we die by following rules or mandatory attendance at church, but to reconnect and repair our separation from God in this present moment. Sin is choosing disconnection rather than the intimacy God longs for with us. God's passion to connect with us is the consistent theme of the Bible.

The Scriptures express God's desire to connect with us and to communicate how beloved we are. As God's children, saved by grace through faith in Jesus Christ, we are assured we are known, loved, seen, forgiven, and adopted by a loving God. God is working in and through us for divine purposes that we might be part of bringing

The deeper meaning of religion isn't to help us earn a spot in heaven when we die by following rules or mandatory attendance at church, but to reconnect and repair our separation from God in this present moment.

The shocking message of the Gospel, seen in the life, death, and resurrection of Christ, is that the doorway to deeper connection and communion with God is through vulnerability and surrender.

My grace is sufficient for you, for my power is made perfect in weakness.

God's light and justice to the world. Abiding in Christ reminds us that nothing can separate us from God's love (Rom 8:39).

Unfortunately, too many of us forget about our divine invitation to be in relationship and get caught up in pressures of making a living, attending to the appetites within us, or the demands around us. Sin is a breach in relationship with God. We make reality about ourselves and lose sight of God's invitation to connection. In trying to keep ourselves from feeling pain, we all learn to put up barriers of anger or withdrawal to protect us, yet these barriers keep us from experiencing the intimacy that we were designed for and God desires. The shocking message of the Gospel, seen in the life, death, and resurrection of Christ, is that the doorway to deeper connection and communion with God is through vulnerability and surrender. There are countless stories in the Bible of flawed people who endure pain and heartache instead of avoiding it, and in doing so discover God more deeply. God is found in our willingness to lean into our fears and pain.

Vulnerability is the bridge to connection. Vulnerability can repair what is divided, if both sides can move toward each other. Jesus is our role model for vulnerability, and therefore he is the great connector. He fully engaged with all his emotions; he laughed, wept, and praised. He was scared and disappointed, and he flipped over tables in anger. He embraced all that life had to offer and, with honesty and humility, turned toward God in prayer to connect. When he experienced the ultimate disconnection, he cried out in anguish, "My God, my God why have you forsaken me?" Yet, even in this moment of torment, Jesus accepted the path of vulnerability and in his last breath said, "Father, into your hands I commend my spirit."

Vulnerability is essential to God's purpose, because in our weakness we must depend not only on God but also on others. Our built-in weaknesses can shift our focus away from ourselves and toward God and others. As Paul reminds us, God loves to help us in our weakness. It is there that God shines, "My grace is sufficient for you, for my power is made perfect in weakness" (2 Cor 12:9). According to God, living with vulnerability can be a threshold to true intimacy.

Our human relationships often parallel our spiritual relationships. Take a moment to reflect on the quality of your prayer life. Do you tell God what you think God wants to hear, while hiding your deepest shortcomings and vulnerabilities? Or like many of the psalms, do you honestly pour out your mind and heart and risk sharing the highs and lows? Do you plead, yell, laugh, and cry? God wants all of us, not just the parts that we think are doing well. God promises to deliver light in darkness and wants us all to follow Christ's example of whole-hearted living. Being more intentional and present with God and others means greater engagement and enjoyment of life. Life is fuller, and we feel more fully alive. We come out of hiding with God and others, and know we are loved and accepted for who we are, warts and all. That freedom allows us to grow and move boldly into the call God has for us.

> God wants all of us, not just the parts that we think are doing well.

If we play it safe and hide our vulnerability, then engagement, the key to connection, will dwindle. It is a challenge to keep our hearts alive in a world that can bruise and break them. As C. S. Lewis writes:

> To love at all is to be vulnerable. Love anything and your heart will be wrung and possibly broken. If you want to make sure of keeping it intact, you must give it to no one, not even an animal. Wrap it carefully round with hobbies and little luxuries; avoid all entanglements. Lock it up safe in the casket or coffin of your selfishness. But in that casket, safe, dark, motionless, airless, it will change. It will not be broken; it will become unbreakable, impenetrable, irredeemable.[3]

It is risky to love and be loved. We will inevitably experience grief and loss. However, like Christ's Way of Sorrows, this is the path to the abundant life and to the riches of God's glorious inheritance. God is eternally waiting to meet us, and those we love, wherever we go—the high road, middle road, and especially the low road. We are invited to be honest about our lives, with ourselves, God, and our spouses. It is our part to risk reaching out and grabbing God's open hand.

For Reflection and Discussion

1 When you consider your most important relationship(s), what is your relationship GPS telling you? Are you off track (disconnected), recalculating (repairing), or arriving at your destination (connected)?

2 As you think about your own style of relating in intimate relationships, do you tend to be more of a withdrawer or pursuer?

3 What have you learned about yourself in reading this chapter that you would like to do differently to improve your relationships?

4 How does God's invitation to relationship impact your view of God and yourself?

5

Finding Home in Our Families

Where It All Started

FROM OUR very beginnings, we were born into and dependent on an intricate web of family relationships. As we have shown, our brains get in sync and allow us to co-regulate our immune systems. Children need high degrees of emotional engagement from their parents because they are not yet capable of self-soothing. They need a wiser, stronger adult for a safety net and to help them regulate their emotions. Sadly, some children who are abandoned or in environments that lack nurture are missing this vital connection. Babies in the first few months are only able to focus their vision up to eighteen inches away. This is the perfect distance from the mother's breast to her face. The baby has all she needs to know visually about her environment when safely held in her parent's arms.

This need for emotional connection isn't just a good thing that enriches our lives; it is critical to our survival. Time and again, research shows that healing is found in relationships and connection with others. As a species, we are not born strong with big claws and teeth. Instead we enter the world totally helpless. Our greatest asset as a species is our ability to bond together and take care of each other. This ability to bond demands people do more than merely protect babies. They must invest time in helping babies know who they are and how relationships work. Children who do not receive emotional engagement from others even when their physical needs for food and shelter are met not only fail to thrive, they can literally die. Some readers may be surprised to learn that we need another's responsiveness as much as oxygen to survive. By our human design, God emphasizes what matters most: relationships. Even baby Jesus, who entered this world and was then laid in a dirty manger, was peacefully reliant upon the loving responsiveness of both his heavenly and earthly parents.

Almost all of us have seen the miracle and gift of a newborn. Maybe we have held our own child or grandchild, a niece or nephew, or a friend's baby. We are awed by the child's neediness and trust in us. As delightful and delicate as children are, they usher in a wild new ride for their parents. Child rearing has a way of revealing to parents that they are no longer the center of anything. This new stage of the parents' lives requires a yet unattained level of selflessness and sacrifice. Children open up new places in our hearts, a love we didn't know we were capable of experiencing. A child can propel most parents, on their best days, to learn love in a whole new way. Nothing grows us like love, and this stretching helps us know God as the divine Parent who will do anything for God's children.

Think of a child who is important to you. What do they teach you about living with hope or play? Parenting and other close relationships with children can bring incalculable joy. Children delight in discovering their world, in earnest abandon to play, and in open-hearted expression of whatever they are feeling or thinking. We also delight in our child's success and ability to overcome life's inevitable trials. I (Heather) was so proud of my daughter Alyse, whose perseverance, hard work, and doing what she had doubts she could pull off led to her getting the female lead in her school play. She had a few challenging rehearsals, which caused her to question the director's and committee's decision to cast her in her part. She even worried she would need to back out with only a few weeks to go till show time. Knowing all that went into her getting on stage opening night, I felt such joy and pride. I was aware that at her age, I would have not had the courage to do what she did. She risked failure and she delivered.

> Children open up new places in our hearts, a love we didn't know we were capable of experiencing.

These are the good days. We all have suffered the hard ones as well, the tears after bullying, the shouts of "I hate you!," the loss of something our child holds dear. All these memories are so powerful that we carry them forward with us, both the positive and the negative. Even now as I write about that wonderful night, I can feel the warmth in my chest and the smile on my face as I replay Alyse singing and shining with passion on stage. Connection is a gift that keeps on giving even after the event passes.

Our focus in this chapter will be on parent/child relationships, but we believe you can apply these principles to most family relationships. Every family relationship is unique, and every family has its own particular culture. Certainly, a single parent, sibling relationships, or blended families have structures, needs, and challenges different from a traditional nuclear family. We encourage our readers to get curious about their distinct family dynamics while also recognizing the basic, universal needs for love, vulnerability, and responsiveness found in every family relationship on this planet.

Disconnection

While some of us delight in the legacy of our families, others spend much of their adulthood trying to overcome their past. Sometimes tragic things happen in what was meant to be our safe haven. When I (Heather) was a young adult, a friend shared a dark secret. Her older brother had raped her repeatedly when they were growing up. I remember the feeling of horror that came over me for what she had experienced. Her brother was strong, mean, and threatening. I couldn't imagine anyone strong enough to stand up to him, especially not a child. As I have had the privilege over the past twenty years to hear more people's stories, I have realized there are many bullies and abusers who take what was not theirs, blame the victim, leave huge heart scars, and cast a pall over others' lives. Abuse is selfish, damaging, and destructive. Families can be a place of secrets and trauma, as much as they can be places of healing and wholeness. We need to see what goes wrong in families in order to understand God's design for redemption.

There is no rulebook for how to get through being a child, sibling, or parent without hurts, bumps, and bruises along the way. Whether we sign up for a parental role, including stepparent, adoptive parent, or foster parent, we get all that life has to bring. What makes the job so complicated is that a parent must flexibly attune to their child's constantly changing needs. To connect, a parent has to be ready to meet their child on whatever road they stumble upon. On the night of Alyse's play, I had to be ready to join her on the high road of accomplishment, the middle road of "it was no big deal," or the low road of failure and humiliation. Luckily, we joined on the high road on the night of her performance. Had her fears won the day, it could easily have been the low road. That is a lot of territory for a parent to cover.

Despite the best of intentions, often parents show up on the wrong road. Imagine the disconnection if Alyse had a terrible performance, and instead of joining her in the disappointment of the low road, I tried instead to pull her up to the high road by celebrating her efforts and success in getting the role. That would have left Alyse alone on the low road. As parents, we have an important responsibility to help our children understand how to deal with their feelings, vulnerabilities, and challenges. A parent who avoids the low road teaches their child to do the same. Failure of a parent to respond appropriately causes a child to lose sight of where they are because they are disconnected from what they feel and do not form a healthy sense of self.

It is easy to respond and love our children when they excel, but often when they need us the most is when they fail. When failure happens, most of us isolate, avoiding the very thing that could make us well. We try to remind our clients that at the end of the day, what matters most isn't the event but how we handle the event. We may not realize it, but all adults—who have begun to think about their

There is no rulebook for how to get through being a child, sibling, or parent without hurts, bumps, and bruises along the way.

lives, emotions, and choices—have a choice to handle the event alone or in connection. Which option we choose makes all the difference.

When I (George) was driving home after an exciting football game in which my son Dylan scored the winning touchdown, our family was in high spirits. Our car was filled with big smiles and laughter as we recounted the thrilling highlights. As Dylan enthusiastically described catching the winning touchdown, I interjected the fact that Dylan actually ran the wrong play, and we got lucky it worked anyway. As his coach, I sometimes can't help pointing out mistakes in the hopes of correcting them. Like a balloon popping, my comment totally changed the dynamics in the car. Instantly, Dylan stopped talking and his brother, CJ, decided to put on his headphones. Shaking her head, my wife, Kathy, said, "Really, you have to bring that up now?" Feeling ganged up on, I defensively replied, "What's the big deal? I'm just trying to make him better. It's ridiculous how sensitive you all are. Dylan just needs to learn how to take in my helpful information and move on." As you can see, this conversation dropped quickly from the high road to the low road in a few seconds.

I tried to repair, telling Dylan, "I'm sorry. Let's get back to talking about that great catch." As you might expect, he declined. The more he refused to engage, the more I pushed. To ease the mounting tension, Kathy jumped in and reminded me of our agreement to not talk about the game for two hours following the end of the game. I guess I broke that rule. Regardless, I let Kathy know I thought that was a stupid rule anyway. When Kathy took out her cell phone, silently joining our sons in protest, I felt incredibly frustrated and utterly alone. That twenty-minute ride home felt like an eternity.

Like couples, family members fall into predictable patterns of disconnect that cause members to protect themselves by either angrily pushing for responsiveness or pulling away to avoid conflict. Pursuers puff themselves up while withdrawers tend to shrink, both strategies designed to influence our environment. Both moves offer

It is easy to respond and love our children when they excel, but often when they need us the most is when they fail.

excellent short-term protection against the pain of disconnection but at the cost of creating more distance and mistrust in the relationships.

When the Faller family arrived home after twenty minutes of silent driving, I was fuming. My calm therapist brain went off-line. Stuck in righteous indignation, I called for a family meeting to pontificate on the need to confront our issues. Kathy shook her head and said, "This is probably not the best timing." CJ mentioned he had some homework to do. Dylan dug in his heals and said, "Go for it dad and tell us all how we did something wrong." Ouch, what a little pursuer he is. On a neurological level, when 95 percent of the glucose in my brain is dealing with my hurt, there is little available to see my son's position. My unregulated brain didn't like his painful jab, so I replied, "Listen, Superstar, if you keep up the attitude you are grounded for a week."

Not missing his opportunity, Dylan angrily replied, "I thought you wanted a conversation. You don't actually want to listen, you just want to give us a lecture. I'm not interested in your advice. Why don't you go to work and give a sermon to your clients, who want your advice." Guess what happened to my outrage and righteous indignation? I could never imagine disrespectfully speaking to my father that way, so I yelled, "Enough, you are grounded for a week! Go to your room."

I wish the bad day ended there, but Kathy chose to jump in and added, "That was pretty unfair. You pushed him to talk, then punished him for speaking his mind." I replied, "You always stick up for him and blame me. He never wants to hear anything from anybody. I wonder where he gets that from?" Just like that, we got into our negative cycle. She starts to criticize, telling me I'm doing it wrong, and I put up my walls to defend while telling her she is overreacting. Mr. Failure meets Mrs. Too Much!

As each of us gets more reactive, it increases our need to defend ourselves and reduces responsiveness. Like a bad cold the contagious virus spreads. Sadly, underneath the defensive anger and withdrawal, we are all feeling the same feelings of helplessness, fear, hurt, and isolation. In disconnection, we all drop down to the low road, on which many family members find themselves cut off from connection. Every member is stuck alone in their own dark hole of negative emotions. Tragically, if family members cannot express their vulnerable fears and hurts resulting from a rupture in their connection, then they lose the ability to repair and bridge distance. They get stuck alone trying to survive the low road, never a viable long-term strategy for healthy relationships. The reason families fracture and break up isn't the specific issues but rather the failure to repair the inevitable misses. Instead of flourishing in the glow of safety and connection, too many family members find themselves lost in disconnection.

To make matters worse, we pass down this legacy of disconnection to future generations. Whenever a child experiences the pain of disconnection, they instinctively work to protect themselves. They cry to protest more or withdraw, believing no one cares or will respond. We all learn ways to cope in life to protect our hearts from past hurt, whether it happened inside or outside our home. Those protective choices may have worked well in the short term but can be limiting as adults.

When John was little, he used to hide in the large tree out back whenever his parents started fighting. Many with experiences like John's grow up and continue to "hide" whenever they experience conflict if they don't have some corrective and healing experience of not hiding, being loved and well received. It is risky to try a new behavior, though, especially when it is likely to end in unresponsiveness. Children who grow into parents pass along the misses of their parents. All parents have good reasons for their blind spots. But hope is on the way.

Repair in Relationships

Relationships are like a garden that needs to be tended, fertilized, requiring work and maintenance. Without the right conditions, plants and vegetables won't grow and can't nourish us. Each of us

> We all learn ways to cope in life to protect our hearts from past hurt, whether it happened inside or outside our home. Those protective choices may have worked well in the short term but can be limiting as adults.

needs to understand the right conditions for growth, how to repair in our busy lives when the right conditions aren't possible, and how we miss each other or experience disconnection. It is far more important for our children to see parents as couples who know how to have a respectful disagreement and then to find resolution than to avoid any appearance of conflict. The knowledge that conflicts can be worked through to a better outcome is a needed life skill (which avoidance won't give them). Parents who think they are helping their kids by never fighting in front of them are also never showing their kids how to repair. Relationships are living, active, fluid, porous, and ever-changing. If we don't understand the fragility of relationships, or the need for constant maintenance and awareness of the relationship, we will find ourselves off track.

It is no big deal to get off track if we can notice and get back on track. To repair and get back on track, we need a map. However, a map is only helpful if you are willing to use it. Refusing to admit you are lost doesn't help. To get better at using maps, we need to change the way we perceive getting off track, so we can change the way we get back on track. Needing a map isn't evidence that we are failing, only an admission of our humanity. Life involves movement, change, stress, and disconnection. Getting lost is part of the natural process of exploring and growing. We need to teach our children how to expand their perspective to see the opportunity in disconnection (getting lost) and the importance of how to repair. But if they don't see what it looks at home, then it is likely they too will get lost without a map.

You can't repair if you either don't notice the problem or you don't have a solution. It is the parents' responsibility to model both understanding the problem and solving it. Let's keep it simple: the problem is prolonged disconnection and the solution is connection. To achieve this solution, parents need to find the right balance between love and limits. Limits are a way love is expressed. Children need both emotional responsiveness and the structure of authority to understand what works and doesn't work in relationships.

> If we don't understand the fragility of relationships, or the need for constant maintenance and awareness of the relationship, we will find ourselves off track.

Often parents over-identify with one responsibility and come up short on the other. An overly authoritarian parent provides lots of structure and rules, but their failure to emotionally attune leaves children feeling unloved. This environment produces children who are good at performing but lack the ability to express their vulnerabilities and have trouble defining their own sense of self.

On the other extreme, an emotionally enabling parent often fails to provide clear and consistent structure, resulting in every interaction being open to the child's feedback and negotiation. Parents saying "no" prepares kids for the necessary disruptions of life and the need to delay gratification. An overly indulgent environment produces children who feel loved but struggle with not getting their way and lack the skills to put others before their own needs.

Children need both emotional responsiveness and the structure of authority to understand what works and doesn't work in relationships.

Identifying whether and how a parent's attention to these dual responsibilities is out of balance reveals the direction in which correction needs to occur. If you are leaning heavily in the limits and discipline category, then opening up your heart to be impacted by your child's vulnerability will pull you toward comforting and supporting. If you are inclined to overprotection and immediate responsiveness to your child, then learning to tolerate the discomfort of your child's distress about not getting what they want will push you toward getting better at saying "no."

An attuned parent has the most flexibility to move fluidly among the three different roads. Authoritarian parents flourish on the middle road but often struggle on the high and low road. Enabling parents tend to do well on the high road but run into difficulties on the middle and low road. Neither strategy enables parents to show up on the low road. If parents don't connect on the low road, then their children will learn to go it alone and hide their pain and feelings of inadequacy from others.

The good news is relationships can withstand lots of tension and pressure, as long as family members can repair the misses. Life throws us all hard days and difficult challenges. It may be the death of a loved one, bullying in school, a move, or a challenge our child is facing that seems like the proverbial straw that breaks the camel's back. All of us experience some frustration, disappointment, feeling neglected or misunderstood along the way. That is because we are fallible and aren't in control of all that comes our way. Perfection is not attainable, and finding peace with the messiness of family life can go a long way toward creating space for healing. That is not to say there aren't plenty of things to repent of, learn from, and grow beyond. We can change, thank God. The problems we're facing can be worked through if we take the right steps to remedy them. Repair not only fixes but strengthens our relationships with one another.

Good-Enough Parenting

Here is a question to help evaluate parental job performance. What percentage of the time does a parent need to correctly respond, with the right balance of love and limits, to a child's need for that child to go on and develop what researchers call "secure attachment," the healthiest of attachment styles, one characterized by trust, openness, and curiosity? Before you guess, we have another question: what percentage of the time does our culture and the pressure of those around us expect us to correctly respond to our children's needs? Most of us put immense stress on ourselves and other parents—to get as close to 100 percent as possible. The surprising answer is parents only need to get it right 30 percent of the time for their child to develop secure attachment.[1] We only have to be "good enough," as psychotherapists describe what is needed. You probably feel relieved—and surprised—to read that the best parents get it wrong more often than they get it right. How is this possible?

Humans are incredibly resilient creatures, and our emotional resiliency takes into account the high probability of disconnection. Parents have good reasons to miss signals: They get too busy, distracted by many others and their own needs. Sometimes the to-do list has to get done or your best friend is in a crisis and needs to talk immediately. Good-enough parents make many mistakes,

Parents only need to get it right 30 percent of the time for their child to develop secure attachment.

Good-enough parents make many mistakes, but the one thing they excel at is repairing (responding correctly).

As children mature, they need to figure out things on their own and have their parents take a step back.

but the one thing they excel at is repairing (responding correctly). When the misses start to mount, good-enough parents recognize the distance growing in their relationship, and they demonstrate how to repair by putting their child's needs first. An attuned parent notices the child's growing defensiveness or withdrawal and understands it is as a natural response to disconnection. Instead of overreacting to the child's self-protection, secure parents attempt to add the missing ingredients behind the acting-out behavior: attention and responsiveness, and structure and support.

A helpful concept practiced by many good-enough parents is "connecting before offering advice." From the time children are born, parents are thrust into the role of being the expert who knows what to do. When a child eats, sleeps, and plays is decided by the parent. To be good at their job, parents need to know how to give orders and motivate their children to "do the right things." Children need their parents to be wiser than they are and to know what to do. Every time a parent pushes their child to behave in a desired way, it reinforces the parent's role as expert. It doesn't hurt that this position as the leader with lots of knowledge and experience provides parents with a great deal of satisfaction and meaning.

Yet, as children mature, they need to figure out things on their own and have their parents take a step back. This is difficult for many parents to do, because they know better and want to help their kids succeed. Despite the research saying giving advice in relationships is effective only 10 percent of the time, it makes sense that parents find it difficult to not give advice. Offering guidance seems like the fastest route to fix the problem, but it is rarely appreciated by the receiver. Many parents do not realize that when they start with advice, they are indirectly (or maybe even directly) delivering a message that the other person is doing something wrong or can do better. If our children are looking for corrective feedback (do these kids actually exist out there?), then leading with advice is perfectly attuned. If they are looking for connection and support, then advice is usually way off the mark. Instead of turning toward the advice giver, kids usually turn away.

In the Faller family car debacle, I (George) was able to repair later that night. After calming down, I recognized how my advice was poorly timed. I got the order out of whack by giving advice before I connected. No one wants an evaluation of their performance when they are soaring on the high road. I knocked on Dylan's door, and when he said to "come in," I proceeded to run in and jump into the bed with him shouting, "My dad is so annoying." As we playfully wrestled, I told him I was sorry. The last thing he needed to hear while celebrating a victory was my advice. I told him I was proud of how he expressed himself, and I too hated when my parents used to critique my efforts, then get annoyed at my protests. I guess the apple doesn't fall too far from the tree. Dylan laughed and then surprised me by asking about the wrong play in the game. I chose intentionally to not give advice and instead stayed in the intoxication of connection and repair.

NAME IT in Action

A blended family has its own unique challenges. I (Heather) believe God's gift of my journey, the highs and lows, has expanded my heart to better understand how others struggle and the opportunities for heart expansion to extend the definition of family. I have been married with a child, divorced when my daughter was two years old, a single mom for four years, and a stepmother and wife for the past eight years. Being a stepparent, one needs to work to find a role; one needs patience, time, and faithfulness. Stepparents need to remember that your spouse chose you, but the children had to receive you. Their lived experience is different from yours. Yet, to form a new family, there are still parent/child dynamics that need to be established and maintained for the system to be as healthy as possible. When Mark and I were married, my daughter was six years old, and his two children, Catie and Douglas, were sixteen and nineteen respectively. I couldn't be more blessed to be a part of my husband's and all three children's lives. But as parents, we had to be thoughtful about how to address the needs of a kindergartener, which were different from those of a teenager, as we formed our new union. One incident shows how we repaired a disconnection in a NAME IT fashion.

Within our first year of marriage, Mark and I became aware of a dynamic that we wanted to address. Because Alyse was with us the majority of the time, she was the one who also pushed back the most on the changes that a new marriage and family bring. She could get angry and be less respectful of Mark when he chimed in, to support my efforts, about needing to go and get ready for bed. As many children feel when their parent remarries, she didn't appreciate having a new person in her life telling her what to do. One night, she was so angry that she told him in strong terms, "You are not my daddy! I just want to be with Mommy again." Mark angrily threw up his arms and walked away.

I remember feeling torn in that moment. I knew that she was hurt and angry, but I also wanted our home to be one of love, peace, and respect. How could we get there from here? As a mom, who will always feel sad and upset that my daughter had to suffer a divorce at such a young age, I wanted to protect her from her pain. Mark was a reminder that her own biological father was not in the room. However, Mark was a part of her life on a daily basis and was helping to raise her. He was only assisting me to help her get enough sleep and was not being overbearing or unreasonable in his words or tone.

After she marched up to her room, Mark and I spoke of the challenging position he was in and what it felt like for him. He told me, "This is tough for me. I try to be supportive and caring, but when she dismisses what I have to say, it hurts. I feel like I am failing at what I am trying so hard to get right, and it makes me want to give up. I completely understand how upset she is, missing her own father and seeing me as an interloper, but her anger and disrespect are hard to handle. I think it is important for her sense of development that she view me as a parent, but I'm not sure what to do."

I have always credited Mark with high EQ (emotional intelligence). He was exactly right. Mark was able to Notice how he was feeling and to Acknowledge Alyse's hurt and pain. With my help, he was able to recognize the negative pattern they were falling into, where Alyse would get angry and Mark would give up and walk away, causing further disengagement. The mistrust and distance were growing rapidly in their relationship. He was able to hold both truths and see how they were getting polarized (Merge). Mark was ready to initiate repair.

As he and I spoke, I realized that I had been too permissive in not reinforcing loving limits for my daughter, because I was trying to protect Alyse from feeling bad. I knew how much she needed her sleep to feel happy and calm the next day, and I was not being strong enough in helping her achieve that goal. By doing so, I was setting Mark up to fail, because he had to fill the gap.

I went first to Alyse and spoke of why Dad was reinforcing the need for bedtime, that this is what good dads do. I said, "I know you miss your Daddy and I am sorry about that. It makes me sad with you. Dad isn't here to replace your Daddy, but he is a new parent, and you need to treat him with respect just like Catie and Douglas treat me with respect. It is part of being a family together."

She was in a calmer place, and we agreed to have Dad come up to say "good night." When Mark arrived, he told her he was sorry that she was upset with him, that he wasn't trying to take the place of her Daddy, and that he wanted to help her get her needed sleep. He also explained that when he walked away, it was because he loved her so much, and he didn't want to cause a bigger fight by getting angry back. He told Alyse, "I now understand how my walking away doesn't work so well. When you are angry, it is because something is really important to you, and you need me to listen. I will do a better job of listening to you."

With his kindness taking the lead, she was forgiving and willing to apologize for not listening and doing what was asked of her. To my surprise, Alyse also recognized their negative cycle and said, "Dad,

I'll try harder to really let you know what is bothering me instead of getting angry and pushing you away." They hugged (Embrace), and then I joined them for a three-way hug. The positive feelings that came for all of us Integrated their two truths and their desire to honor their newly forming relationship.

That night started a weekly Tuesday-night tradition where Mark and Alyse chatted together before bed. I spoke my word of Thanks to both of them: "Thank you two; this makes Mommy's heart happy. I love you both so much and am glad that you are learning to love each other too!" The many moments of repair over the years have threaded our five hearts together as a new family. I couldn't be more grateful.

Experiencing God in Families

Our families, on the good days and difficult ones, can be a place to get to know God better and to experience God's heart for us as parents and children. The gift of families is that we have an opportunity to see God at work in and through us—as parents, children, or spouses. There is nothing like being a parent, grandparent, aunt or uncle, or child's caregiver to help us get a glimpse into God's heart for us as God's beloved children. God is the ultimate Parent. On our best days, we reflect something of that loving intention and unconditional loving kindness to those in our midst. We want to share a few stories of how as parents we have experienced God more deeply.

For me (Heather) this was true as I checked in on my teenage daughter one night after she fell asleep. As I saw her face illuminated by the dim hall light, something happened for the first time. I saw her profile and was reminded of a headshot of her from an ultrasound when she was in the womb. *This* was the *same* face. That tiny face had grown into this young lady's face. All the wonder of loving her back then before she breathed her first breath came back to me. I reviewed her past fourteen years and how that love

> The gift of families is that we have an opportunity to see God at work in and through us—as parents, children, or spouses.

continues and grows as she becomes even more her own person. I was overcome with gratitude for the gift of being her mother.

The next morning, I was in a contemplative prayer group, one woman prayed for us as "God's daughters." Tears came to my eyes as I suddenly realized that the joy, pride, wonder, and delight I felt as my daughter's parent was the same way God sees me, looks at me and all of us. God's love is the perfect expression of parental love—absorbing all our hurts, suffering, and pettiness into God's welcoming embrace. If we have eyes to see and ears to hear, we find glimpses of the holy in the ordinary all about us.

For me (George), meeting on the low road when life brings us challenges is less scary as a member of a family, because I know I'm not alone. I remember a few years back our old dog Zoey (thirteen years old) was having a bunch of seizures and losing weight. We figured it was serious and we'd probably have to put her down. Our whole family spent the morning saying goodbye to Zoey before the dreaded noon appointment at the vet. All four of us cried while sitting around Zoey and gently rubbing her fur. It was so painful, but we were in it together. It was my sons' first real experience of losing someone they love, and it broke my heart to see their agony.

On the excruciating drive to the vet, Dylan prayed for a miracle. I remember telling him, "I think God is ready to call Zoey back home to him. Zoey lived a full live, and she's ready to run in heaven."

At the vet's office, my boys wailed, saying their final goodbyes as Kathy and I left them in the waiting area to head into the surgery room for euthanasia. We held each other close as we waited for the veterinarian to finish his examination and bring an end to Zoey's suffering. I'll never forget the doctor's unusual expression when he turned to us and asked, "Have you ever heard of old dog syndrome?" Turns out Zoey's seizures were not life-threatening, and it was likely she could live a couple more years. We were free to take her home with some vitamins. We opened the door with Zoey alert in my arms and told our boys she was coming home. Dylan screamed out, "I have the luck of

> God's love is the perfect expression of parental love—absorbing all our hurts, suffering, and pettiness into God's welcoming embrace.

the Irish, and I knew God would answer me!" In that innocent moment, my family joined together in a mush pot of tears, smiles, and laughter, surrounded by the real presence of God's love. Like my children, in that moment I felt I was truly home.

It is amazing when the sadness and pain of the low road surprisingly turns into the joy of the high road. Yet, this happy turn OF events isn't necessarily the norm. Even if there is no avoiding the hurt of the low road, though, there is always the opportunity to find connection in the pain.

Fast forward eighteen months. Zoey was close to fifteen years old, and she was struggling to breathe and get up. This time there would be no miracles. As we tearily drove to the vet, we said our goodbyes and thanked Zoey for her years of love and unfailing dedication. With broken hearts, we watched her last breath and experienced the profound agony of disconnection that loving well brings. For me as a parent, seeing my children's hurt was excruciating. I had my own sadness to deal with in losing my loyal companion, but watching my sons for the first time question whether the risk to love is worth the inevitable pain only compounded my devastation. Together we wept, and together we faced the pain—and doing it together made all the difference. Zoey was gone, but we still found our way toward each other, and the low road brought us to the same destination as the high road: home.

Redeeming Our Past by Becoming Like Little Children

As parents, we can learn more about the heart of God by being students of our children. We can learn so much from children about freedom, play, openness, and honesty. Jesus invites us "to become like little children." In his ministry, we know of at least one scene when children came right up to him. They weren't afraid or worried about cutting in line. They were drawn to him and sensed his strength and kindness. For me (Heather), one story stands out as a picture of grace from my experience as a parent. The first scene took place on the beach of the Outer Banks in North Carolina when Alyse was three. This was her first encounter with a big wave beach. She ran into the shallows and started to twirl, skip, leap, and dance. Her actions were spontaneous, pure, and innocent. Without knowing the words to the song, she was so moved by the glory of God's creation that she had to respond. As her mother, I saw strong waves, riptides, and a fierce undertow. She saw, felt, and responded to the beauty of the earth. She danced with the waves. Let me ask you: Would you be fully comfortable jumping and twirling in the air on a beach without concern for who might be passing by or seeing you, even moving out of your way? (I wouldn't be.) Why not? What gets in our way? What lessons has life taught us that inhibit our freedom?

I believe this picture shows us how we were meant to be. What holds us back is social conditioning; the world's sin of consumerism, independence, and competition (making us feel inadequate, isolated, and disconnected); and our own sin of self-focus, busyness, and entitlement (diminishing our ability to engage with God in us). We were meant to be dancers in God's glorious creation, but hurt and harm along life's path shaped us and took away some of our sense of freedom and spontaneity. My daughter, in her play, reminded me of the childlike faith and trust that Jesus invites us to embrace.

Perhaps better stated, parenting and helping invest in the next generation, honoring families of birth and families of choice, can be an opportunity to unlearn false ways of believing, living, and trying to control our world. We can experience a release to freedom, passion, hope, and worship by observing and imitating our children's unselfconscious expressions of joy and faith. Sounds inviting, doesn't it? We are not fully in control. Thankfully, we can trust our Creator has more in store for us than whatever present suffering we are enduring. Let's get our dancing shoes on and embrace the healing and redemption we can bring to and find in our families.

There is nothing like parenting to transform our very being to one that loves more like God loves. Study after study shows that strong

We can learn so much from children about freedom, play, openness, and honesty. Jesus invites us "to become like little children."

Study after study shows that strong relationships are the best predictor of a happy and fulfilling life.

> Regardless of our difficult experiences, we are hardwired for connection, repair, and responsiveness.

relationships are the best predictor of a happy and fulfilling life. These findings are consistent across all races, countries, ages, genders, and social classes. The predominant place where we form strong relationships is within families. It is where we discover love and connection. No matter how far away we get from our families in space or time, we carry them with us always. Obviously, families are at the center of God's heart.

Many parents discover the grace to support their children in ways they never received in their childhood. How can a parent who was continuously abused and neglected in childhood lovingly comfort their child's pain? This ability to give as parents something we didn't receive as children is proof of the powerful longings God created in all our hearts to love and respond to vulnerability. It is our natural language infused in every breath. Regardless of our difficult experiences, we are hardwired for connection, repair, and responsiveness. A parent is designed to be God's messenger on earth, lovingly embracing their child regardless of all their unworthiness. In every parent-child relationship, we get to witness redemption at work. Whatever road life takes us down, when we look closely into each other's eyes, we can also catch a glimpse of the face of God.

For Reflection and Discussion

1 In what ways can you relate to the disruption and repair cycle in your family relationships?

2 In your family of origin, what was the balance between love (emotional responsiveness) and limits (authority and discipline)?

3 What is the balance of love and limits in your current relationships?

4 How have children—your own or others—brought you glimpses of God?

6

Leaning into Loss

At the heart of all losses is pain and disconnection.

The Pain of Loss

MOST OF us buy into the creed that adding things to our lives makes us feel better. We assume adding a new car, friend, or vacation enriches our lives. Conversely, loss is unwelcome and involves taking things away. Losing turns the world into an unfriendly place. There are many types of losses, ranging from the frustration of simply losing our car keys to the devastation of losing a child. We can lose a possession, like our house; status, like our job title; something internal, like our health; or something relational, like a person close to us. All losses, especially of someone we love, undermine safety and security while they usher in waves of agony and helplessness. At the heart of all losses is pain and disconnection.

I (George) will never forget the dreaded 4:00 a.m. phone call I received a few years ago when I was away working in Seattle. My father had suddenly and unexpectedly died of a heart attack. I couldn't breathe as my mind raced with a million crazy thoughts. How could this happen? My heart broke when his heart stopped beating. With mounting dread, I knew the source of so much good in my life was undeniably gone. In a flash, my foundation disappeared and was replaced with fear, uncertainty, pain, sadness, and isolation. I was almost three thousand miles away from the man I always believed would be there whenever I needed help. Now I was alone with a huge hole in my life. For years, I have felt like the terrible news that knocked my breath out is sitting on my chest, making it difficult to take deep, full breaths.

Disconnection from someone we love puts us on a roller-coaster ride, swinging from intense feelings of torment to feeling nothing at all. For many people, the aftermath of loss is worse than the actual event. To endure, we need to protect ourselves. Most try to avoid the pain by distracting ourselves with work or turning toward something else to help us cope with the pain. Inevitably, this replacement connection—to alcohol, drugs, TV, food, gambling, porn, shopping, or whatever other false hope brings temporary relief—creates long-term problems that exacerbate the disconnection and loss. The escape only lasts so long before inevitably the loss comes back with a vengeance. Racing thoughts, replaying memories, and what-if questions bombard our mind with uncontrollable and unrelenting frequency. It feels so unfair that all the effort and investment put into that relationship is gone and never coming back. Many people feel they are going crazy because they can't stop their brain from focusing on the loss and what went wrong. No wonder in their desperation people turn toward anything that can bring them relief. Yet it is impossible to outrun the pain. Eventually it catches us all.

Learning to Embrace the Pain

Christian spiritual formation writer Hannah Hurnard wrote *Hinds' Feet on High Places*. Her protagonist, Much-Afraid, says wise words about relationships that I (Heather) have carried with me most of my adult life: "I have been told if you really love someone, you give that loved one the power to hurt and pain you in a way that nothing else can."[1] Love, by nature of the vulnerability required to offer our heart to another, is threatening. To risk loving is a courageous act. Throughout life, we will lose others through death, divorce, betrayal, neglect, or abuse. When we have entrusted our heart to someone else, it is, in a way, residing outside of ourselves. We cannot keep it from harm. The only possible way to keep our heart safe would be to lock it up and guard it, imprisoning it and

> When we have entrusted our heart to someone else, it is, in a way, residing outside of ourselves. We cannot keep it from harm.

ensuring we will wither and die. We cannot live if we deny any attempt to love. Loss feels catastrophic. Often in the midst of it, we question the sanity that led us to this place of hurt. We can even feel shame for daring to love. However, these broken parts of our heart can be regenerated.

How do we deal with loss that rocks our worlds? Our choices range from getting busy to feeling angry, to numbing out, to withdrawing and isolating—or we can allow ourselves to feel the pain and move through it in time. The last option is really the only healing or therapeutic one, but it requires the greatest courage. All of us are pain-averse and avoidant. Emotional pain registers in the same place in the brain as physical pain. It literally hurts. No wonder we work hard to avoid feeling grief. Over time, the alternate coping techniques we choose to distance ourselves from pain become inadequate. We are blocked from growing and moving on from the loss. If we are fortunate, we will reach a point where we decide to begin facing the pain, often prompted by the concern of those who care about us.

Elisabeth Kübler-Ross's description of the dying process is commonly used to understand loss. The grief process is predictable; we all go through similar stages of denial, anger, bargaining, depression, and acceptance. The key is understanding the destination: acceptance. We can accept when times are good and embrace the present moment. Yet, how do we find acceptance when the present moment is horrific?

The counterintuitive move in dealing with loss is to not flee or fight the pain as it surfaces in our hearts. Rather, healing comes in allowing ourselves to feel the pain. It actually can move through us, and we can find relief. The pain is communicating an important message. It is a constant reminder of disconnection, and its purpose is to push us to reach toward the solution: connection. When we listen to its wise advice, it points us where we need to go. Embracing the pain itself holds the keys to our own healing. Within the pain is an invitation to live and love with even more vitality

> The counterintuitive move in dealing with loss is to not flee or fight the pain as it surfaces in our hearts. Rather, healing comes in allowing ourselves to feel the pain.

and compassion than before. We realize that our ability to find meaningful connections isn't totally dependent on the person who is gone. In the pain are opportunities to find comfort and kindness from others, ourselves, and God.

How do we change our trajectory from coping and avoiding to dealing and embracing? We can pursue many different avenues to rebuild what is broken. We may journal or read the Scriptures on comfort. We may take new actions, like reaching out to friends, praying with our clergy or Stephen Minister, joining a grief group, or seeing a counselor. When I (Heather) was recovering from my divorce and relocating across country with my two-year-old daughter, I utilized many of these avenues of healing. I will never forget the words of my therapist at the time. Lois wisely told me:

> I know you have a busy life and lots of responsibility as a working single mom. As the grief comes, when the time is right, just sit with it. Allow it to be with you. It may be for fifteen minutes. Just let it be. Like waves on a beach, the pain will ebb and recede. It will come in more forcefully at first like an incoming high tide. It will then slowly slacken and every time you experience it, the impact should lessen.

Her words were true in my experience. It was a simple but profound road map for creating the space I needed for the grief while balancing it with the other important demands in my life.

Ultimately, grief is an opportunity—when we are ready to take it. Look back at your times of loss and sorrow. If you are like most people, I imagine over time you came to realize some new truths about yourself and the world. Grief cracks us open in such a way that we can't help but be vulnerable. When that happens, we find we are more porous and open to "God moments," which we might define as the sense that God is drawing near. We also find deeper connections with others who join around us to help us heal and get back on our feet. Grief gives us perspective and clarifies what or who really matters. Often our values are recalibrated by

Ultimately, grief is an opportunity—when we are ready to take it.

the experience. We learn not to sweat the small stuff, because loss reminds us what is most important.

NAME IT in Action

When I (Heather) consider losses I've experienced and look at how God has brought repair to the situations, the elements of our NAME IT repair process are evident in one of my most poignant memories from almost two decades ago. I sat with my mother in a coffee house. I was in my midthirties and felt like I needed to talk about something important with the person I considered my best friend, my mom. Living at a distance made these conversations harder to have, but there was still something that needed to be said to remove an impediment to our closeness. I wanted to talk about my infertility and how it seemed to be affecting our relationship but didn't want to hurt her or open myself open for hurt, even if unintentional.

I had Noticed that when I brought up another failed attempt with medical tests and procedures intended to help me conceive, my mother's reply made me sad, even though she wasn't intending to do so. Typically, she responded with a well-meaning statement of faith that God would work it all out or that maybe we would have better luck next time. She didn't seem to acknowledge what was true for me: I felt terribly disappointed. I know she didn't mean to be dismissive, but I felt like the sorrow I was feeling was not allowed. After disappointing medical news, I wanted to share with her how I was doing, so that I would not put up walls that might dampen our loving friendship. I like to avoid conflict, so telling her that I *felt* dismissed, even if that wasn't what she intended, was risky for me. I also knew my mom had her own perspective, and I needed to Acknowledge that as well. Like me, my mom liked to reassure people and avoid hurting anyone's feelings.

As we settled into our comfortable seats, began sipping our coffee, and paused in our catch-up conversation, I stepped into my fear.

"Mom, I want to talk to you about my infertility. This awful process has gone on many years, and I know it bothers you too, but it's hard for me to share with you about how I am doing with all this."

"I didn't know it was hard. Tell me why."

"Honestly, it is scary to talk about. I feel like sometimes when I tell you I am hurting, you try to make it better. But in that moment, I just want you to be sad with me." (I let her know I wanted connection instead of advice.)

"You are right, I do want you to feel better, but it is because I love you and feel so powerless to help make this right for you. I know how much you want to be a mom. I think you would be a great one, and I am sad and frustrated too." (We had both hidden our sadness from one another, out of love and hoping to not make the hurt worse, but inadvertently we created distance between us. We were now Merging our truths.)

"It really helps to hear you say that. I didn't know you felt that way too."

"Of course. I don't want to shut you down or make you think you can't share important things with me. I love hearing your stories and being in life together." (We were Embracing each other's vulnerability.)

"You are my best friend, and I want to be able to share this with you too."

"Tell me what might be most helpful for you when you call and just got bad news."

"It is okay just to let it be hard. It actually makes it feel like a lightened load knowing you are standing with me in it."

"That is where I want to be. Thanks for letting me know that you were hurting and how I can be in it with you better."

"Thanks so much for listening and talking with me about this. I love you, Mom."

"I love you too. Let's be sure to have our 'coffee talks' even when you are on the other coast, so we can keep the communication channels unclogged."

"I would love that."

By speaking truth to one another, we were able to Integrate our new way of communicating in the moment and commit to continue doing so. That restored intimacy lead to Thanksgiving. We realized this "hard" talk brought us closer and encouraged us to be more honest in the future. The positive resolution felt good for both of us.

It was out of that positive experience that I was able to draw strength to have another heartbreaking conversation with both my mother and my father. It was Christmastime. I had traveled from the West Coast to visit my extended family with Alyse, then one year old, but without my spouse. I knew I needed to step away from the situation I was in and take a few deep breaths before speaking about what was before me. In that space of Noticing what was true (I was afraid of their disapproval if I told the truth about how troubled our marriage was), I decided I needed to be honest with myself and with them. My parents had graciously given me space to not share anything that I wasn't ready to talk about. It was time to Acknowledge what was true for them as my parents and their own reactions to this difficult story.

My parents and I were alone in our family room. I spoke my truth, choking out the words, "I don't know that our marriage is going to make it." I was sitting on the floor as they both sat in front of me on the coach. My body knew what was needed, even though my reaction caught me by surprise; I broke down in sobs and leaned into my mother's lap. My father leaned over, and they both held me. I had been the adult child, trying to be strong and manage the heartache on my own, but that false pride melted away with their arms around me. Our two truths Merged. Instead of my parents being angry and disappointed, they entered my heartache with me.

They were concerned and wanted to help. I had misjudged what their perspective would be (using my own harsh lens rather than theirs, one of compassion). The difference between their real feelings and my misconception dissolved instantly when they held me and poured their love into me. The shift took place without words.

In our Embrace, I was able to acknowledge my sorrow about letting them down, and they could respond, "We are really sad and sorry you are dealing with this. We don't want you to be in a situation that kills your spirit. We love you and stand behind you no matter what."

I told them, "I thought you would be upset or angry with me. I wish this weren't true, but I am so glad to know I was wrong. It means so much to me to know you are in this with me."

They responded, "We are so glad you came home and that you shared what is on your heart. You are not alone. We are with you and will be praying for you."

We Integrated our new understanding of what was true between us. And all of us were able to express our Thankfulness for this new level of honesty and affection.

My parents' grace and love, offered at my lowest point, when I was feeling the most unwanted and unlovable, were like stitches on an open-heart wound. Their understanding began the process, which took years, of bringing healing to me in body, mind, and spirit. This was a powerful healing offering a picture of God's love for me no matter what. They opened their home to me and Alyse and restored a sense of family when we moved back from Seattle after my divorce. Alyse was two, and we rented from them for four years. Their hospitality was invaluable for me in my work as a chaplain, because at various times during three of those years, I was an on-call chaplain for our local hospital and wore a beeper around the clock. With a chaplain's salary, I couldn't have afforded all-night babysitting fees for the times I was paged.

There were many life pearls my parents gave me during those challenging years. The first was the invaluable, yet humbling, lesson that it is okay to grieve and okay to fail. As Romans 8 describes God, they embodied the truth that nothing can separate us from the love of God in Christ Jesus. I also learned not to give up. Overcoming a challenge may feel impossible, but we have to keep investing in life and others. Eventually we will feel better and it will make sense. In other words, we can keep hope alive.

Although the NAME IT process is helpful for repairing loss, we cannot always repair with the one we have lost or are losing. Notice in this story, the mending was with my parents rather than my estranged spouse. But through others entering into my pain, my own healing was begun. My desire for connection with them outweighed my fears and distorted beliefs about how they, others, and God must see me. Our two truths merged. We integrated a new insight for all of us, which was realizing that by being honest with our pain, we were able to find comfort and hope. I learned I could be loved no matter what. I won't be abandoned because I feel unlovable and unworthy. God has written more of my story than this chapter. There will be a tomorrow. Those are truths all people in grief must learn. Often God uses relationships with others as the vehicle to communicate that to us. We need to look out for the "helpers" who are already in our story, and then we can take the risky move of sharing our hurts and hopes with them.

Different Types of Losses

Relational loss comes in many shapes and sizes. Recognizing the predictable steps of grief makes it easier to adopt effective strategies to deal with specific types of losses. Although the pain we experience in all losses is similar, there are differences worth exploring.

We need to look out for the "helpers" who are already in our story, and then we can take the risky move of sharing our hurts and hopes with them.

Divorce

Divorce means a loss of dreams. In divorce, the person meant to be your greatest ally turns into an enemy. Not only do you not get your needs met, but the other person is actively working against your needs. Plans for "happily ever after" crash and burn. The messiness of dividing assets and child custody often turns partners into bitter rivals. Blaming your partner and blaming yourself for the failure of the marriage are both bad options.

For the partner who wants out, there is often guilt and resentment at unmet needs. The partner who wants to keep the marriage but seems to have no choice in letting their partner leave often feels abandonment and longing for all that they hoped the relationship could have been or was on the best of days. Any lost relationship can become idealized, even if there was mistreatment or neglect. Being honest about what was true can help provide both partners relief and freedom to remind each other why they are on this path. Regardless of who made the final decision to end the marriage, both sides do better when they practice forgiveness.

Holding on to resentment and not forgiving comes at a huge price. The anger, unfairness, and bitterness color the world as unsafe and typically lead to withdrawal, defensiveness, and deep loneliness. The key to forgiveness is the realization that forgiving is in the best interests of the forgiver. The decision to forgive is a choice to let go and see the opportunities in the loss. Those individuals who can extend forgiveness experience higher levels of emotional satisfaction and well-being than those who hold on to their justified resentment. It may not be possible to reconcile, which takes two people and their apologies to put in action, but forgiveness is always an option for those who want liberation from the pain of loss.

Illness

Illness is another form of loss, of security and wellness, that can strip us of our daily routine and remind us that we are finite. Sickness affects not only us but also all those around us. We grieve and

> The key to forgiveness is the realization that forgiving is in the best interests of the forgiver. The decision to forgive is a choice to let go and see the opportunities in the loss.

long for the days when we were blissfully ignorant of how blessed we were to feel well, to bounce out of bed with a spring in our step, to think we might live for a long time to come. Humility (and sometimes even humiliation) can be required to accept help from others and face the fact that we are weak. I (Heather) saw diminishing abilities as a challenge for the patients in the hospital and subacute nursing facilities where I worked as a chaplain. It is hard to accept our limitations, especially if this illness presents a new normal for us to adjust to. There may be no going back to the way things were. When our loved ones are sick and not getting well, we need to find ways to support them as they move through grief, anger, discouragement, and even a sense of despair.

Most patients with a serious illness experience many of the emotional transitions Elisabeth Kübler-Ross spoke of as the stages of dying. Ultimately, illness presents the opportunity to find a way to accept and work with what is. We can do our best to change and challenge our illness, but we may also need the words of the Serenity Prayer as well, for "the serenity to accept the things we cannot change, the courage to change the things we can, and wisdom to know the difference." It is a courageous act to work toward a new life and discover new joy and meaning.

> Ultimately, illness presents the opportunity to find a way to accept and work with what is.

Infertility

Infertility makes us feel like we cannot make life work the way it should. Two people fall in love, decide to start a family, and expect they will be successful. For many people, that is not the case. I (Heather) took eight and a half years, the better part of a decade, to conceive and bring a child to term. The treatment process is expensive, often invasive, and requires teams of professionals trying to do the seemingly impossible, make you a parent. The hormone treatments caused menopausal symptoms and often left me feeling sick and despairing. The journey was long, with many tears and unanswered prayers. I lived with an ongoing feeling of sadness inside. I was teaching in graduate school, counseling others, and completing my doctoral degree—living a full life—but there was a hole at the center. In an area that mattered most to me, I was failing.

The infertility journey was one of trying to find meaning in suffering, trying to figure out what hope meant, asking God many questions, and living with those questions unanswered. It was a season of waiting, waiting, and then waiting some more. It was a roller-coaster ride of possibility and more bad news. For some, the end result is a welcome pregnancy, others decide to adopt, and others choose to make a new life, one without raising a family at its center. In any case, there is often a great deal of strain and stress on the couple. Ongoing grief and disappointment are wearing on the best of relationships. The grief can be an avenue to a deepened relationship, but it requires the couple to be willing to share how they are doing with not succeeding at this joint task. It requires faith that their relationship and God's love for them outweigh the loss.

Job Loss

Losing a job, identity, or status is excruciating for many who invest so much of their energy cultivating an image to present to the world. Countless hours are sacrificed to position ourselves in the right spot with the right people. Achieving our goals results in feeling safe and fitting in. There are many relational consequences of job loss. Families may have to move, another family member may need to work or work several jobs to keep their heads above water. As the unemployed person finds more closed doors when seeking new positions, their sense of self-worth and ability to act in a meaningful way in the world are threatened. At the same time, their spouse may be disappointed and frustrated, only reinforcing their negative self-concept. Depression or despair can be outcomes for some. Other family members are impacted financially, relationally, and emotionally. For some, job loss means the loss of social standing, which can turn the world upside down. Sadly, for some, death is a better option than being downsized. It is humiliating to be seen as publicly failing and rejected by your desired group. As with all losses, the healing lies in embracing the pain and learning to get clearer

> The grief can be an avenue to a deepened relationship, but it requires the couple to be willing to share how they are doing with not succeeding at this joint task.

> As with all losses, the healing lies in embracing the pain and learning to get clearer on what is most important.

on what is most important. Is it the money and lifestyle you miss or the attention and affirmation the job afforded? We believe soul searching in the pain sheds light on healthier ways of feeling seen and valued.

Death

Finally, there is the ultimate loss, death. Death is a final separation, where all that was good is over and all that was unfinished can no longer be completed, at least as we think it might have been. A radical altering of our knowledge of self is required as we learn to live a life without that person who held so many memories with us, knew our secrets, and may have had bigger visions for us then we had for ourselves. We need to learn to accept our new life with a hole in it, an ache that can change but will not disappear. There is no right way to grieve, but it is abundantly clear that regardless of how we do it, those who do the best in the grieving process learn to embrace the pain instead of numbing it out. Riding the wave of pain pushes us toward the shore and new beginnings, rather than leaving us adrift at sea.

The Redemptive Doorway

Although the sources of the loss vary greatly, the destination of acceptance and rediscovering connection is the same. Loss is the ultimate reminder of the importance of love and connection. We are born into connection, and despite the temporary interruption to connection caused by the loss, our end point, reached with our last breath, is oneness with those we love and our Maker. Pain, no matter how protracted, is just a temporary state. In the darkness of an ending, we believe the light of God becomes clearer. God created us with love, and nothing we do can separate us from that love. At times, we may doubt this truth, but love is much stronger than our hurts and fears.

Recently, I (George) presented at a conference on the benefits of vulnerability and connection. At the end of my presentation, an old

> There is no right way to grieve, but it is abundantly clear that regardless of how we do it, those who do the best in the grieving process learn to embrace the pain instead of numbing it out.

> God created us with love, and nothing we do can separate us from that love.

man came up with tears in his eyes to shake my hand. He said, "For the past few years since my wife died, I have been silently suffering in resignation to my fate. Your talk awakened a longing in my heart. I want more than waiting for death. I have so much more inside me to give, I just needed some permission to go for it." As we shook hands, he smiled and out of nowhere said, "Wow, your dad must be proud of you." Immediately, I felt a wave of warmth and a tingling sensation. In that moment, I felt the connection with my dad. I knew with certainty that he was watching how I use his love to encourage others to follow their hearts. With moist eyes and a smile, I said, "Thank you for your kind response. My dad is no longer alive, but your words allowed me to feel his presence today." For the first time in years, I took in a full, deep breath filled with the comfort of his love.

A God of love uses bad things to bring about good. There is no denying the sheer agony of loss, but the good news is the story doesn't end there. The disconnection may end a chapter in our lives, but there is another chapter to come. Recognizing that loss isn't permanent makes it easier to accept. Trusting instead of avoiding the pain, trusting the pain to lead us home to connection, is a promise worth believing.

An antidote for our losses is being able to see the place of redemptive suffering in the life of faith. Scriptures describe God working in all things for good. However, that may take time, longer than seems just to us, and might not necessarily feel good along the way. God's design is to repair the damage relationships suffer and to give us a new perspective on our daily struggles and disconnections.

How are we meant to go through the sufferings and losses life brings? Scripture offers us an image of faith-filled lives. In Psalm 112, we learn that people of faith will find light even in darkness and are like God in being gracious, compassionate, and righteous. They are generous, lend freely, and act justly. We are told they will never be shaken. Their hearts are steadfast and secure. Trusting in God they will have no fear, and their righteousness endures forever. This

> There is no denying the sheer agony of loss, but the good news is the story doesn't end there.

theme resurfaces in Isaiah 26:3: "You [God] will keep in perfect peace all who trust in you, all whose minds are fixed on you." These people of faith seem to have found the secret, the path to the abundant life. They live fully and generously without fear because they are anchored in God.

For those who open their hearts to understand their own grief—and invite God and others into that vulnerable space—we discover that in our weakness, we are strong. When we listen to what we feel without judgment, when we acknowledge difficult emotions like shame, anger, or sadness without correcting ourselves or denying and suppressing what is true, we can stay calmer and be honest and real with others and God. Vulnerability means sharing what is true about our story with another. We can know and be known when we take the mask off and let others in, whether we feel triumphant or defeated. Vulnerability is the connection with others and God that can make us more resilient, grounded, and unflappable. Even when we feel unlovable or hopeless, we can overcome our isolation if we move toward others in it. Do you see how counterintuitive some of this is? Sharing the very parts of us that feel raw and unlovable with those who are safe and close to us can strengthen our relationships. We fear vulnerability will repel people, but ironically, it does the opposite. It deepens the connection, and we can receive love and support when we need it most.

For many of us, letting others see our weaknesses may not be something we are particularly good at. We may be great when it comes to juggling many demands, achieving success, getting a lot done, keeping our children challenged and scheduled—but speaking the truth of our hearts and souls does not always come as easily. We are not alone.

But what if we viewed our present challenges differently and saw them as opportunities instead of obstacles? If we viewed our struggles as doors that open toward learning new lessons and interacting with others in a new way, we would change our story. As we listen more deeply to our truth about our hearts and what we

For those who open their hearts to understand their own grief—and invite God and others into that vulnerable space—we discover that in our weakness, we are strong.

feel, we can choose to move toward others we trust and be honest about how we are and what we are dealing with. The support and encouragement we receive on the other side will convince us tenfold that our risk was worth taking.

We don't seek out suffering, but when we encounter it, we work with it, pray through it, and allow it to not only transform us but, in so doing, become a catalyst for growth for those around us. It can help us to bring healing and justice to a fractured world.

People of faith have a deepened capacity for resilience and vulnerability. Most of us on good days believe that we were created by a loving God who cares for us, knows us, journeys with us in life's ups and downs, and has given meaning and purposefulness to the universe, even if we haven't found it yet. We recognize a security that lies beyond us, the light the psalmist is pointing to. We can see loss as an opportunity for growth, not a disease or death sentence.

Another line of poetry from the Psalms speaks to the hope we have that God will find us in our distress. "Out of my distress, I called on the Lord; the Lord answered me and set me in a broad place" (Ps 118:5). This tells us God cares for each one of us and knows what we are feeling, thinking, worried about, hoping for, doubting, and longing for. We are promised that when we are hard-pressed, when we feel discouraged and overwhelmed, we can remember there is a God who cares about us, who will join us in the struggle, and who will open a spacious place. This pressure will be lifted, a cool breeze will blow, and there is hope for a better tomorrow than today. We will then look back on what we went through and see the hand of God leading and guiding. We can be people who are not shaken, who aren't afraid of bad news, because we are audacious enough to risk trusting in the unseen God who allows us to be steadfast, sure, confident, and firm no matter our circumstances. We find our hope in God, who will give us a foretaste of that spacious place that awaits.

Through grieving what was lost, being humbled by circumstances, receiving others' love and support, and finding a deeper walk with

> We can be people who are not shaken, who aren't afraid of bad news, because we are audacious enough to risk trusting in the unseen God who allows us to be steadfast, sure, confident, and firm no matter our circumstances.

God through the losses, healing slowly emerges from the darkness. For me (Heather), healing the loss of my marriage began with seeing that God loved me unconditionally, regardless of my status. I began to trust that no matter my failures, in God's eyes I am worthy of love. As my heart expanded, I felt ready to risk again. I met a wonderful man, Mark, whose faithful pursuit of me and desire for my best, along with his strong intellect, kind heart, and great parenting skills, won me over.

For me (George), the losses of friends on 9/11, my brother, and my father revealed to me that faith is not limited to what we believe is going to happen when we die but is the way we live right now. God wants to engage with us in the present moment, and pain is often God's doorway to reach us. For me, Psalm 34:18, "The Lord is near to the brokenhearted, and saves the crushed in spirit," comes viscerally alive whenever in my mind I see the faces of those I lost and realize I am not alone. God is patiently with me in the tears, knowing the tears will turn to laughter someday soon.

Through the doorway of loss, we are invited to find God waiting on the other side, to meet the one Being who actually accepts, loves, and delights in us, even in our dark places. Certainly, when we cannot find God in times of need, the rejection hurts, and its normal to harden our hearts after disappointment. Yet, nothing can be worse than choosing isolation and no longer hoping to connect to a world beyond us. The good news of the gospel is that regardless of our choice, nothing we can do will ever separate us from God's love. Connection is God's intention and ultimate plan for all of us. When we think of the power of loss and disconnection to send trauma signals to the brain and pain to our hearts, this message brings light into the darkness. It is God's offer to join us in a relationship. God guarantees to be with us on whatever road we walk. In the midst of the brokenness, infertility, divorce, death—God is.

Our confident message, strengthened by both experience and clinical research, is that the only way we can keep our hearts open to the pain of the present moment is to trust there is connection

> Through the doorway of loss, we are invited to find God waiting on the other side, to meet the one Being who actually accepts, loves, and delights in us, even in our dark places.

coming beyond our current loss. It may take months or years to believe, but loss is not the end. There is always a new beginning in the eternal dance of connection.

Are you ready to get back on the dance floor and dance?

For Reflection and Discussion

1 In what ways could you see grief as an opportunity?

2 What methods have you used to overcome your past losses? What new ones might you try from this chapter?

3 How has God drawn near and shaped you as you have moved through your losses?

7

Discovering Community

IMAGINE THIS scene. Parents head into their teenagers' high school to volunteer their time and help coordinate the school's annual fundraiser. All are united in supporting their children and the school. A good-natured discussion starts around how much involvement in running the activities is expected from the students. Some parents feel strongly that the students need the freedom to unleash their entrepreneurial spirits and use this opportunity to learn from their successes and failures. Others vehemently object, complaining that the goal of the fundraiser is to make money, and it is the staff and parents' responsibility to vigorously manage the students to ensure success. The universal good intentions of all parents quickly deteriorate into name-calling and accusations. One group replies, "This is what is wrong with America, too many rules and regulations"; to which the other group replies "No, what is wrong with America is irresponsible selfishness in disguise as doing-the-right-thing." In a flash, collaboration is replaced with confrontation, leaving the school staff with the unpleasant task of trying to manage irate parents who are supposedly there to help the school. With help like this, is it any wonder why some schools want to eliminate PTA meetings?

In our society, civil debate and discussions seem nonexistent. Some say we have lost a public square where it is emotionally safe to disagree, argue toward a better solution together, and find truth. It is easy for all of us to be with those we agree with, but what about finding ways to deal with difference? That can be a worthy goal to work toward in our lives and communities.

Much of the work we do as therapists, especially with couples and families, but still indirectly with individuals, is around dealing with conflict. After writing *Sacred Stress*, we were on a number of national radio shows in the fall of 2016 and were asked often what we do about the conflict people were experiencing in their marriages before and after the election. Marriages faltered and people needed counseling to weather their feelings about the election outcome. We know we need each other, but sometimes our differences seem insurmountable or irreconcilable—is there even a path back? How many wars are fought between parties who are both convinced that they are right?

We seem to have lost the ability in our families and in the public sphere for honest debate and dialogue. What do we do when we feel silenced because our views don't match those of our tribe? Many retreat into themselves or wear a false mask to appear to go along with the majority view, whatever that might be in the moment. Both of us have done it too. Over time, if disengagement and hiding become our only way of relating to those who don't agree with us, we become isolated and lonely. We know ourselves as we are known by others. Poor engagement with others leads to alienation from self and can harm our physical and emotional health. We need others and God for our personal health and well-being. As we feel more distant from ourselves, it becomes harder to reconnect with others. The uphill climb becomes even steeper as we seek the medicine most needed for personal and relational repair.

No wonder our society is the most anxious, depressed, heavily medicated, and addicted on the planet. We have a chronic problem of disconnection and loneliness. Connection matters. When it is lost, people suffer. One such example is evidenced by our returning military veterans. When they are away at war, they experience high degrees of bonding and engagement with their fellow soldiers. They

We know ourselves as
we are known by others.

discover a level of closeness and cooperation that life-and-death situations often produce.

Certainly, I (George) can relate to this scenario with my fire department experience. The bond is so tight you will die for each other. Almost every moment at war is spent in the company of others—eating, training, working, fighting, laughing, crying, and sleeping. Soldiers experience joy and struggle together with high degrees of engagement. The elevated levels of oxytocin and dopamine resulting from so much connection feel great, despite the hardships. Then when the tour of service is over, we attempt to give veterans rest by disconnecting them from their peers and sending them off into a community that doesn't function with this level of connection and cannot really relate to their experience. Talk about hurtful help.

Imaging being a soldier and trying to readjust to life back home. Instead of constantly being around others, now you may be with people but alone in your lived experience and memories. The energy expended to keep yourself and others alive at war is now redirected to important things like watching TV and going shopping. So much of domestic life loses its luster when you have experienced the high levels of connection in combat. Choosing which fast-food restaurant to dine at pales in comparison to the bonding of sharing delicious MREs (Meal, Ready to Eat) after battle or a long day on patrol through contested terrain. Soldiers don't miss the war; they miss the closeness they found at war and that they can't find back at home.

This disconnection is a recipe for PTSD, divorce, addiction, violence, and suicide. Not surprisingly, the mental-health statistics for returning vets are frightening. Currently, the US military has the highest rates of PTSD in its history. We are treating a social problem of disconnection as an individual's illness—or at best, as an issue unique to the military. No wonder the rates of PTSD keep rising.[1] As our country's social groups continue to grow smaller as we choose larger houses and more stuff over human connections, our health suffers. Entertainment and material things cannot replace the responsiveness of family, friends, extended family, peers, social groups, and civic endeavors.

Compare the US military to Israel's military, which boasts very low levels of PTSD, despite chronic threats and fighting. How is this possible? We are relatively safe, while they are constantly at war. How can they suffer less PTSD on average than US soldiers? Israel uses the community to mitigate the effects of combat by intentionally reintegrating soldiers into society, with an emphasis on maintaining closeness and mutual understanding.[2] We believe PTSD, like addiction, depression, and a whole host of other mental health problems, is really a symptom of persistent disconnection. We have lost our way as a society, and we need to redefine what is most important if we want to reverse this trend of isolation.

The Possibility of Community

The answer to this health-shattering disconnection sounds almost too simple: we heal our communities by returning to our roots and reestablishing the importance of relationships. Most people report that when they've been through tough times, "angels of mercy" came alongside them and offered them aid. I (Heather) think of the mover wearing a Catholic University sweatshirt who helped me collect my salvageable belongings after the first floor of our home was flooded in Hurricane Sandy. His simple and soft-spoken words, "God bless you," were like food in a famine. I felt great relief that a stranger offered a brief prayer for us in our travail through those simple words of compassion. A light was shone in the darkness, when we were the most vulnerable. When it was hard for us to think straight, let alone pray, the faith of others carried us through the storm.

Both of us (Heather and George) have been rescued by others from a number of difficult passages in our lives. We are so grateful for those friends who knew how to offer words of encouragement,

We have lost our way as a society, and we need to redefine what is most important if we want to reverse this trend of isolation.

> In current struggles, whatever they may be, it is good to recall times God raised up people to support us. We may be called to do the same for someone else in our lives. Does anyone come to mind for you that you could be community to now?

comfort, and a helping hand and who were aware of what we needed even more than we were. They were lifelines. We trust that as you look back over the course of your life, names and faces come to mind as your helpers in times of need. They were the picture of true community at work.

I (George) will never forget how the cheers of others kept me going after September 11, 2001. For many people, their recollections of September 11 end with the collapse of the second tower. For most first responders, the nightmare began at that moment. It was demoralizing to work all day, trying to find survivors only to find death and destruction. As the chances of finding anyone alive dwindled to zero, the work grew much more challenging. Even the search-and-rescue dogs started getting depressed when they couldn't find anyone alive. Ground Zero became a desolate tomb that disheartened most who entered. We breathed in smoke from fires that never went out, smelled the decay of dead bodies buried too deep under rubble to find, and robotically staffed the endless bucket brigades trying to remove the never-ending pile of debris. No one complained; we had a job to do. But the negativity at times felt oppressive.

One day while searching through the debris of the World Trade Center, we discovered the dismembered legs of a fallen firefighter, the rest of his body still missing. I remember feeling dread and revulsion at the thought of telling his wife the news. How would I tell this dead hero's wife we found only his legs? In that moment, I questioned how much more of this I could take. I felt exhausted and beaten down.

After taking the body parts to the morgue, we headed back to our bus to go home—our heads down, feeling hopeless and defeated. That's when the applause of thousands of people lined up outside of Ground Zero to cheer for the rescuers as they finished another day on the site helped breathe fresh air of hope into my deflated spirit. Witnessing people of every color, age, and religion come together and stand as one to support us and the nation was truly inspiring. Focusing on our common humanity and shared sorrow, the unified group provided us with much needed energy. Their appreciation gave us renewed purpose when we were most dejected. I still, after all these years, get goose bumps recalling how those perfectly timed cheers gave me a dose of love that I desperately needed to keep going.

We are not designed to deal with fear, pain, and tragedy alone. Although the months after 9/11 often felt like the worst of times, they also brought out the best in people. Looking back, I (George) can honestly say I never felt more connected to the larger community than I did during those few months. People were nice, accepting, tolerant, full of grace, and willing to look out for others. Sometimes it takes a disaster to remind us all what is really most important.

Unfortunately, it seems too difficult for many of us to hold on to those hard-fought life lessons following the collapse of the World Trade Center. Our common humanity has again splintered apart into tiny fractions of competing truths. Instead of finding leaders who excel at connection, we are finding leaders who excel at creating separation.

The spirit of this book is captured by our simple belief in the value of holding two truths, our own and that of someone who sees the world differently than we do. Honoring both sides of a debate requires holding the tension between opposites, not to force someone to be like us but to respect how diverse discourse invites both sides to grow. Our professional practice has taught us to reconcile seeming opposites and the value in standing in the space between two truths. It is entirely possible and enriching to hold together my view and yours. As the world gets smaller

We are not designed to deal with fear, pain, and tragedy alone.

Honoring both sides of a debate requires holding the tension between opposites, not to force someone to be like us but to respect how diverse discourse invites both sides to grow.

and our differences get magnified, this ability to make room for opposing viewpoints is even more critical for us as individuals and as members of a society.

Often people who experience misunderstanding, bullying, discrimination, and hardship develop a greater sensitivity to the importance of making room for difference. We call them bridge builders. They likely encountered situations where people were are not acting in loving or respectful ways to one another, and they want to be change agents. To have new conversations, we need to ask ourselves, Are we willing to see things differently? Can we invite others in a noncoercive way to think differently?

For an image of expanding our view and learning to see differently, we need only look to our astronauts, who in their photos and accounts bring back a new view of life on planet Earth. Scientists have studied their reactions to seeing Earth from space, which include ecstasy and awe, and call them the Overview Effect. Space shuttle astronaut Don L. Lind described the experience: "There was no intellectual preparation I hadn't made. But there is no way you can be prepared for the emotional impact. It was a moving enough experience that it brought tears to my eyes."[3] Soyuz 14 cosmonaut Yury Artyukhin said, "The feeling of unity is not simply an observation. With it comes a strong sense of compassion and concern for the state of our planet and the effect humans are having on it."[4] Not all of us will alter our perspective through space travel, though, so how can we see differently or change our perspective?

We (George and Heather) have been asked to speak to groups and congregations about helping bridge gaps between people who hold different beliefs. Many congregations are caught in the challenges of determining where they stand on social, political, and economic issues, from gun control to immigration, to sexual orientation and ordination. Many risk losing members if they espouse one position or another in what often seem to be polarized and heated debates. We scoff at the idea of an NPR-listening conservative. We can't imagine someone watching both CNN and Fox News. The world

> To have new conversations, we need to ask ourselves, Are we willing to see things differently? Can we invite others in a noncoercive way to think differently?

of today seems myopically focused on black-and-white allegiances. You are either like me or are against me; there is no grey middle ground.

Either/or propositions are different from Biblical values. The Scriptures prescribe a different worldview—one of loving service, caring for others, restoring the broken, giving power to the powerless, and making things right as agents and ambassadors of God's reign on earth. How often does that vision overshadow the ones that surround us every day? We would do well to remember the words of Henry Wadsworth Longfellow: "If we could read the secret history of our enemies we should find in each man's life sorrow and suffering enough to disarm all hostility."[5] If we saw each other as persons with histories that have shaped us—our worldviews and the choices we make—we might find greater tolerance and feel greater compassion toward others. We might adopt the worldview taught in the Bible.

But can our congregations offer a large enough tent that a Libertarian, a capitalist, a Communist, and a Socialist can come to worship and serve alongside one another? If we can't do so in our churches, establishing a spirit of tolerance and mutual respect with a desire for bridge building, it will be much harder in other institutions and areas of our lives. Is unity possible in the face of great difference? We believe it is. One person shows us how to bring many truths together and hold out a hand to everyone.

A young boy in New Orleans, grandson of slaves, abandoned by his parents, sang on the streets for money. A Jewish family, the Karnofskys from Lithuania, had compassion and decided to take him in and raise him as their own. They taught him Yiddish and Russian songs and gave him his first instrument. What he learned in their home—language, culture, and music—shaped who he become. He wore a Star of David for the rest of his life. This boy was Louis "Satchmo" Armstrong. When he and his band played in East Berlin during the Cold War, they decided it would be good after their set to go out for drinks in West Berlin and drove to Checkpoint

> If we saw each other as persons with histories that have shaped us—our worldviews and the choices we make—we might find greater tolerance and feel greater compassion toward others.

Charlie. They were surprised when the car was surrounded by machine-gun-bearing guards and they were forced out of the car. They must have felt some terror about what might happen next. But then one of the guards recognized Louis and called out, "Satchmo?" The guards immediately put their guns down, got autographs, and waved his car through their checkpoint every night the band played in East Berlin. It makes us wonder, how did his story and background prepare him to be a friend to the world, one who never met a stranger? How did he learn to integrate differences and become a global citizen?

NAME IT in Community Restoration

To effectively bridge two truths, we need to remember that just as a person's behavior always makes sense to them, so too do their beliefs and values. As we reach out to build bridges, there is the chance the other person will not respond well to us. If the other side won't engage, we are likely to become defensive. Relationship healing needs both sides to be willing to take a risk.

Let us take a look at how the NAME IT process can help two opposing groups come together. When thinking about a relevant example, we thought, what could illustrate the process better than a fictional conversation between two polarizing figures: Donald Trump and Hillary Clinton. The derision between the two is so palpable and contagious that it has spread across America like a plague. Couples are divorcing, kids are not talking to their parents, and neighbors are moving away because they can't believe someone they know supported the person they can't stand. The decision of a national leader is an important one and speaks to our values, but it is still interesting to consider the fact that people end relationships with those they love because the other person voted for a stranger neither one of them will ever meet.

Our example might seem unbelievable. As a disclaimer, we recognize that a conversation requires two people who are both willing to listen and to be changed by what they hear. A

> Relationship healing needs both sides to be willing to take a risk.

conversation is not possible if either side refuses to engage or accept responsibility for their part. If you think either Donald or Hillary is incapable of such consideration, you may be right. The NAME IT process depends on people having some level of self-awareness, respect, and empathy. However, we believe the possibility of reconciliation is vital to opening up dialogue between all people. Changing the tenor of public discourse in our nation depends on our finding a way to bridge differences and engage in genuine conversation. Too many people are avoiding difficult conversations by surrounding themselves with people and news coverage that support their particular point of view while disparaging those who think differently. This avoidance may prevent escalation in the short term, but in the long term it will prevent healing and reconciliation. As a community, we need to hold out for the possibility that two provocative and polarizing figures can find common ground. Without that as our starting point, we are doomed to separation and divisiveness. We will never find a bridge by staying in the isolated comfort of like-minded groups, refusing to engage with those who seem so different from us.

Now that we have offered our rationale and disclaimers for this scenario, we invite you to suspend your skepticism for a few pages and imagine the NAME IT model applied to a conversation between Hillary and Donald.

One year after her election defeat, Hillary begins the NAME IT process by Noticing how her anger and resentment is only getting worse with time. She desperately wants closure, peace, and happiness, and yet the constant negative news flashes make a ceasefire seem impossible. As Hillary takes in a deep breath, she notices the constant tension she carries throughout her body, signaling her sense of helplessness and her fear that she has no good options. All of her attempts to be heard by asserting her points are her way of trying to create change, but unfortunately they fall on deaf ears. Underneath her anger at Donald's decisions, Hillary feels scared about the future and sad so many people are hurting. Let's

> As a community, we need to hold out for the possibility that two provocative and polarizing figures can find common ground.

return to those key three questions of the Noticing step of NAME IT. After any contact with Donald:

- What does Hillary feel? Angry, sad, misunderstood, and helpless.
- What does she do? She fights back.
- What does she want? To make things better.

Although conversations with Donald never go well, Hillary recognizes that their constant fighting is only exacerbating the country's problems. What she is hoping for, to make things better, is not happening. Understanding the good reasons for her criticism of Donald but also aware of the costs—more reactivity and ill-will—Hillary courageously faces the growing distance between their truths and reluctantly decides to initiate a new, more vulnerable conversation with Donald. Sitting on the beach during her Florida vacation, Hillary reaches out to Oprah to set up a clandestine meeting between herself and Donald at a nondescript coffee house.

Getting clearer on your truth is a good starting point for dialogue, but to build a complete bridge requires awareness of two truths. Armed with greater awareness of both the good intentions of her anger and the vulnerable fears and sadness underneath, Hillary begins the conversation with Donald by curiously exploring and Acknowledging Donald's defensive actions. She admits, "I know we are both frustrated at all the negativity and want what is best for our country. I know what some of the issues concerning me are, but I want to know more about what is upsetting you."

Donald, with a surprised look on his face, says, "Well, Hillary, this is really a thankless job. I'm doing my best and all I get is criticism. I want to make things better, but no one pays attention to my accomplishments. They just repeat the same old misinformation. It is really unfair, and when someone accuses me of intentionally hurting others when all I'm doing is fulfilling my campaign promises, I just want to explode." Going back to the three Notice questions after an interaction:

- What does Donald feel? Angry, misunderstood, misjudged, and helpless.
- What does he do? Fights back.
- What does he want? To make things better.

Wow! Look at how similar his answers are to Hillary's.

Hillary responds calmly and with openness. "I want to make sure I'm getting this right. When I or others criticize your actions, you want to explode and point out to us the errors of our ways. Regardless of the topic—immigration, the wall, health care, taxes, or terrorism—you believe fighting back gives you the best chance at success. That makes sense to me because I do the same thing. You fight so hard because you care so deeply about making things better and not letting down those who believe in you. Your anger and contempt are your way of not letting others hurt you. The best defense is a good offense."

Donald looks confused. He isn't sure what to do with Hillary's validation of his anger. No one ever tells him they understand his temper. As she applies the technique of "connecting before offering advice or giving her perspective" (discussed in chapter 5), Donald starts to relax and lower his defenses. He says, "I have no choice but to attack. If I don't fight back, then everything I worked for will fall apart. Some days I worry that all of this work is for nothing." Exhaling loudly, Donald shakes his head and much to Hillary's surprise, looks down at the floor, saying softly, "Sometimes it's exhausting."

As they both shift the level of communication away from the specific issues and toward their vulnerable feelings, they begin to see each other from a new perspective. Hillary responds with a laugh, "It's ironic that we are so far apart on the issues, but underneath we share such similar feelings—misjudged, worried, helpless, and discouraged. I never could see past your anger and insults, but now I'm starting to see something different."

As Hillary starts to hold both truths and put their moves together (Merge), their negative cycle of self-protection becomes apparent. The more each of them attacks, the more dangerous each appears and the more the other person feels the need to hit harder, so as not to appear weak or soft. Both hope their anger is going to get the other person to listen and motivate them to change, but all it does is get the other person to dig in their heels deeper. As they pass the angry hot potato back and forth, everyone loses. As both parties expand their understanding, they see that by fighting to fulfill their dream of making the world better, they are actually making things worse.

As both Hillary and Donald accept responsibility for their self-protective steps in the negative dance, they create an opportunity to work together instead of against each other. Donald, responding to Hillary's validation of his experience, says, "So, your anger is your protection too? I just figured you hated me. But you also feel discouraged by the negativity?" Hillary, nodding yes, says, "Absolutely. I let a lot of people down by losing the election, and I feel so guilty. I want a chance to make things better, but I feel totally helpless to do anything positive. Constantly running into roadblocks and negative spins makes me feel little and insignificant. I guess the whole thing is massively disappointing." Hillary closes her eyes while shaking her head and leans back in her chair.

Donald, noticing the hurt in Hillary's voice and again surprising her, replies, "I'm sorry you are in such a tough place. All I saw was your angry complaints, and I had no idea you felt so bad. After all your years of service, you deserve respect and a say in what is happening." Smiling, Donald says, "I want to help make things better. It will probably improve our job performance if we support each other instead of knocking each other down. What do you think?" Hillary, smiling back, says, "Yes, I think together we can do a much better job of showing everyone that our love for our country is stronger than our differences. Thank you for your openness, and I hope I can help reduce some of those negative messages, so you don't feel so discouraged. I believe you are trying your best, and as our president, you deserve support, not detractors."

Donald responds with a laugh, "Wow, this is different. Building each other up instead of tearing each other down. You know how much I love building things, although this mutual cooperation is going to change the tone of my daily tweets."

As Donald and Hillary connect in their vulnerability (Embrace), their responsiveness to each other creates a positive cycle to replace the negative one. Even after years of fighting, every disagreement holds the potential to transform the disconnection of fighting into the repair of connection for those courageous enough to seize the moment. Embracing each other's vulnerability allows them to merge their mutual desire to make the world a better place instead of working against each other.

With a wide grin, Donald jokingly replies, "I guess I didn't see this coming. Maybe I'm not as smart as I think. How can we make this right?" As the two brainstorm to Integrate their positive experience, they decide holding a joint press conference would be a good start. Both also recognize there is no shortcut to building trust; it is earned through the hard work of spending time together. So they agree to meet once a month, thinking getting together is a good start in that direction.

To complete the NAME IT repair process, Donald and Hillary take a moment to explicitly Thank each other for the risks and responsiveness necessary to make this momentous shift happen. Together they held two separate truths, and in doing so they revealed a deeper, unified truth. Like so many of us after 9/11, Donald and Hillary realized that we are so much stronger together than apart. Mutual respect and grace create more space to hold differences while also reminding us of the unbelievable power of our common humanity.

Mutual respect and grace create more space to hold differences while also reminding us of the unbelievable power of our common humanity.

Bridge Builders

OK, some of you may be thinking this conversation is a stretch. Our hope is that NAME IT empowers our readers to envision the possibility of repair in every situation, no matter how dismal it may appear. However, if we can't imagine a repair conversation between our leaders, how is it ever going to happen? If we can imagine the possibility, then we can put pressure on our leaders to follow our lead. Shouldn't we expect our leaders to be experts at repair instead of confrontation? It is in our best interests as a society to demand that anyone in a leadership position demonstrates an ability to hold two truths simultaneously. Using the NAME IT process can help us to foster connection instead of divisiveness.

Bridge builders know what to do when opposing sides are separated by an ocean: they help both sides recognize the choice to either swim together or sink together. Choosing to live in our small camps while creating enemies out of those who see things differently really limits our worldview and breeds disconnection. We need to challenge our assumptions and figure out what is so threatening about diverse viewpoints. If something is really true, then we should not be alarmed if others see it from a different angle. When we learn to see the big truths that unite us all, it is easier to see how the small truths are just limited interpretations of particular experiences. The key to bridge building is found not in blind allegiance to our own experience but in actually walking in another person's shoes. The capacity to reconcile in relationships is rooted in empathy and the ability to mutually feel together. As a society, it is vital to our very survival to envision the possiblity of polarizing figures finding their shared, common humanity underneath the disconnections. If we do not accept and vote for those who sow discord, if we instead support bridge builders, then we open up the possibility that our leaders will represent the values we hold most dear. Regardless of the topic, we all face the same choice: do we treat those with whom we disagree as enemies or as fellow members of our community? The choice determines whether our society heads in the direction of health and connection or hostility and discord.

> Regardless of the topic, we all face the same choice: do we treat those with whom we disagree as enemies or as fellow members of our community?

Spiritual Significance of Community

With a healthier view of relationships, we can begin developing broader communities of connection that fit God's design for us, the church, and the world. Our heart of compassion can expand as we realize what healthy relationships look like and how they benefit all creation. As God's agents, we are invited to participate in bettering the world by learning to listen and love well.

Community can be a profound gift and a vehicle of grace. Like the lawyer who asked Jesus to summarize the teachings of the law, we are commanded to first love God fully and completely, and then to love our neighbor as ourselves. Our obedience to this command, we believe, is where we will find the greatest sense of joy, fulfillment, and purpose as people of faith. In community, with God and others, we find who we are meant to be and accomplish what we are uniquely invited to do to make God's world a better place. Embedded in our faith tradition are key components to healthy living together as the body of Christ. Those that enhance relationships—the ways we live and flourish in community—include confession, fellowship, justice and mercy, and peacekeeping.

> We need to challenge our assumptions and figure out what is so threatening about diverse viewpoints.

Confession

We often hear a client in a conflicted marriage say, "My spouse will never apologize." Why are the words "I'm sorry" so hard to say? For some, apologizing represents failure or weakness, both of which are taboo when it comes to their view of self or how to make life work. Owning our mistakes is a humbling task and one that means putting the other person and the relationships before our need for self-protection or "looking good." We believe confession is an antidote to isolation because it causes us to turn toward God. We confess in church each week, because loving relationships— ours with God, as with others—invite and depend on honesty and repentance. Confession is the door to restoring our relationship with God and others. We recognize what we have done and what we have left undone. We ask God for forgiveness from our sins, debts, or trespasses as we forgive those done to us. While these are personal words of contrition, we often speak them aloud together. It is a communal act. We sin personally and corporately, and we can forgive personally and corporately as well.

Fellowship

Our clients often feel isolated in their secret struggles. The best outcomes for our graduating clients happen when they are part of broader community that they can reinvest in and that will support them. This can be a network of friends, family, or a faith community. When clients request it, we work with clergy to help integrate that person back into their congregation. People can get plugged into service projects, join groups, and receive clergy or lay pastoral care.

The Hebrew Scriptures highlight the importance of understanding the self as a part of a collective identity, the people of God. In our modern lingo, we would say we are all in this mess together. The self is also understood as part of a family. "As for me and my household, we will serve the Lord," we read in Joshua, a statement of faith that begins with a web of relationships. We speak for and represent one another because of our affiliation.

Christian community at its finest is a place of generosity and sharing. The book of Acts tells of the mutual concern and attention that early Christians had for one another. Whoever was in need was provided for. Like an extended family, the church cared for one another without question. In fact, those who held back but pretended to be more generous than they were met with an unfortunate fate. We are in communion with each other and share one with another. Christ's words, "All people will know that you are my disciples, if you have love for one another" (John 13:35), show the Christian life is evidenced by love. We know from the witness of Jesus that this love is sacrificial, other-centered, and participating in others' stories, which impact our own.

All people will know that you are my disciples, if you have love for one another.

Justice and Mercy

As counselors, we hear many painful and difficult stories. Our hearts go out the victims, and we try to comprehend the brokenness and pain of the people who inflict hurt and harm on others. We are compelled to be people of mercy but, at the same time, to champion justice for the brokenness within relationships and our society. We believe all Christians, not just those in helping professions, are called to practice mercy and justice.

The biblical concepts of *koinonia* and *mishpat* add to our understanding of what community is meant to be. *Mishpat* is one of the Hebrew words for "justice" but implies more than we usually think of. It is about God's judgment *with loving kindness*. It is power and mercy combined. We see *mishpat* used in Micah 6:8: "He has told you what is good and what the Lord requires of you, to do justice [*mishpat*], to love mercy [*hesed*], and to walk humbly with your God." Justice is action taken to bring God's kingdom, God's right order, to our world and our places of influence. As one seminary president put it, "There is strong evidence that originally *mishpat* referred to the restoration of a situation or environment which promoted equity and harmony in a community."[6] How exciting for us to be agents ushering in God's good intentions for this world. We are part of the plan enacted through our participation.

When we work to bring God's *mishpat* to the world—setting things right, helping the oppressed, caring for our neighbor—the reign of God is made real and manifest. In our words and actions, we embody God's love.

Peacemaking

When a couple moves from mistrust and anger to connection and intimacy, we get to witness a miracle of healing right in front of us. The opportunity to be used by God to facilitate peace and love where there was conflict, shame, and hurt is why we do what we do.

How exciting for us to be agents ushering in God's good intentions for this world.

All people of faith can grow internally in *shalom*—in peace and wholeness—as we work as peacemakers with others.

All people of faith can grow internally in *shalom*—in peace and wholeness—as we work as peacemakers with others. We are invited to be reconcilers, to bring back into right relationship those who are disconnected, marginalized, outcast, or considered untouchables. Jesus invites us in the Sermon on the Mount to live a faith-filled life, promising, "Blessed are the peacemakers." If each of us chose to be peacemakers in the relationships closest to us, the ripple effect would be global. Mother Teresa once said, "Spread love everywhere you go: first of all in your own house. Give love to your children, to your wife or husband, to a next door neighbor."[7] Those words are simple but profound and a wonderful invitation to be change makers in our own communities for the good of others and our own souls.

God's call to be peacemakers isn't easy to respond to in a world that likes to pick sides, drawing distinctions between the good and bad guys. There are too many hostile camps convinced they are right and the other side is morally bankrupt and stupid. Replacing honest conversation with the blame game leads to many people talking but no one listening. Many of us don't recognize that our refusal to acknowledge the truth in others slowly hardens our hearts and warps our perspectives. Sadly, arguing over small truths only widens the divide and intensifies defensiveness. Before long, stereotyping leads to dehumanization. Our United States are in discord rather than union. We need a bold approach that turns away from separation and toward accord. The American Friends Service Committee advises that in resolving conflict, loving our enemies may be met with resistance and seem to fail, but the Spirit of love will prevail.[8]

It is insane that there is so little education provided to our children at home and in school about the value of connection and how to repair. We are allowing our kids to "wing it" and then get surprised at their poor results in expressing their emotional needs. Our society cannot afford to continue giving our attention to the importance of connections only when there are problems. If everything else is a priority and our relationships get only get the little amount of engagement we have left at the end of a long day, then guess what? Our relationships are going to struggle. We must honor our Maker by committing to placing relationships and community at the top of our priority list. Heading away from connection—for individuals, nations, and humanity as a whole—is a recipe for disaster. If we accumulate all the wealth in the world but have few connections, then we will live in spiritual poverty. We believe that God's invitation to love and connection with God and others is the real "truth that will set you free" (John 8:32). In love, we become part of something much grander than our narrow worldview. God's great truth, accessible from many different vantage points, overcomes divisions and assimilates the many into one diverse, rich whole.

For Reflection and Discussion

1 When have you become disconnected from a community that was once important to you? What would you have longed for in that disconnected place?

2 We invite you to think of an issue, maybe social or political, that really matters to you: gun control, immigration, health care reform, terrorism, abortion, and so forth. Do you know someone who is on the opposite side of the issue from you? Consider what a conversation with that person might look like if you were to try the NAME IT process with them. Pay attention to the resistance that comes up as you imagine doing so. How might you move through those blocks?

3 Which spiritual practice do you think might deepen your faith in community? What steps can you take to move into that area now?

God's invitation to love and connection with God and others is the real "truth that will set you free" (John 8:32).

8

Encountering God

THIS BOOK highlights God's simple plan for relating, the love loop. In this circle of life—birth, death, rebirth—connecting, disconnecting, and repair are all essential ingredients to health and growth. As we follow this circle, we encounter ups and downs on a universal road leading to our home, union with God. Learning to courageously embrace this unavoidable love loop relieves from us the pressure of trying to be in control and masters of our destiny.

God wants to be in a dynamic relationship with us right now, not wait around to evaluate our impeccable resume at the end of our lives. When we understand the purpose of the love loop is continuous deepening of the union, then we also recognize that nothing we do can separate us from God's love. As painful as disconnection can feel, it is just a temporary interruption until the inevitable return to connection. Regardless of the chaos and turmoil in our lives, one thing remains constant and unconditional: God's love as demonstrated in Christ's life, death, and resurrection on our behalf.

One thing remains constant and unconditional: God's love.

In every disconnection, God gives us the chance to grow and more clearly see this reality: God created us and everything else to be in true connection. We can choose to stay in the distress of separateness, releasing cortisol throughout our bodies, or we can pick connection and the sweet flow of oxytocin. Everything revealed through God's word assures us of God's everlasting fidelity. God implores us, regardless of our performance, to turn toward God. Faith is more about being connected than being correct.[1] God wants our presence, not our performance, and is open and available to us 24 hours a day, 365 days a year.

Meeting God in the Moment

Unfortunately, although God is available to us, we often are not available to God. We live in a time with access to so much technology, information, and stimulation that slowing down to be present in the moment is extremely challenging. We carry around devices that vibrate, chime, whistle, tweet, and speak, constantly reminding us of things we need to do. The constant distractions keep us busy and performing, seeking success, but at what cost?

The story of the sisters Mary and Martha, Jesus's friends, offers us insight into God's viewpoint on how to best engage life (Luke 10:39–42). Martha, like most of us, is busy doing everyday work stuff like cooking and cleaning, activities necessary to maintain our lifestyle. Mary on the other hand, consciously chooses to put aside the work and instead spend the time sitting at Jesus's feet. Responding to Martha's complaints about Mary's laziness, Jesus says that Mary chose wisely and that Martha has allowed her busyness to interfere with the most important things in life.

How many of us, like Martha, focus our energies on preparing the meal and miss the opportunity to engage in the moment, to connect with Jesus? We spend so much of our precious time worrying about the future or fretting about the past that we allow the important present moment to slip past unnoticed. Jesus wants to free us from obsessing about what could have happened or what might happen. Instead, he wants us to pay attention to the aliveness of what is happening. Reliving the past or worrying about the future keeps us stuck in our heads, disconnected from the now-ness of our hearts, bodies, souls, and spirits. The presence of God is eternally found in the present moment, and God is patiently waiting for us to sit at God's feet.

> Faith is more about being connected than being correct.

Heartbreakingly, like Martha, so many of us waste so much of our valuable time trying to earn God's love by "doing the right things" or worrying about what happens when we die that we deny the connection available in the moment. That is why prayer is so indispensable—because it immediately ends our separation from God and focuses our attention in the present moment, on our Maker. Praying builds a bridge and redirects our attention toward what is most important. In our worries and hurts, we rediscover God's eternal promise to never leave our sides.

To connect to billions of souls, God must be good at coming alongside the uniqueness of each individual. God is the master of holding multiple truths because God understands the deeper, universal truth uniting them all. Imagine two soldiers in opposing armies praying to the same God for help. How can God be present for both? Because God knows that regardless of what happens in the battle, they are both destined to return to the same place, connection with God. God longs for that connection whenever and wherever it comes. In that perfect moment of connection, time doesn't matter as we surrender to Universal Love. And in the process of joining God and others, we don't lose ourselves but actually become part of something more beautiful than our separate selves. The big question for all of us is, Why wait till heaven for this amazing love when it is available right now?

NAME IT with Other Believers and Faith-Seekers

My (Heather's) sense of call began at fifteen, when I journaled about what I would one day do as a minister. This was in response to a particularly vivid dream I had in which I was pulling others up from a dark pit and toward a brilliant light that shone down on us. During this period of my teen years, I grew up in a politically and socially conservative home, attended a moderate mainline Presbyterian church, and had a radical, pacifist, feminist youth minister. She was full of life and defied my understanding of what it meant to be a Christian, particularly to work in a church. I was baffled but intrigued by her. She may have been my first lesson that

God longs for connection whenever and wherever it comes.

walking with God was going to be different from what I might imagine. My journey of faith has been a varied and diverse one. I have been learning to live the NAME IT model to move through defensiveness and fear, to acceptance and love toward those who are different from me.

On this journey, I have encountered and even sought out many people who are not like me. After my university experience, I worked in business, attended seminary, worked in a church, attended graduate school in counseling, and then taught as a graduate school professor while attaining my doctorate in ministry. During the course of my graduate studies, I attended an evangelical seminary, then a mainline seminary, a Christian university, and finally a liberal mainline seminary. I worked for a conservative Baptist seminary's satellite campus in Seattle while attending (progressive) San Francisco Theological Seminary for a doctorate. Neither group trusted me, and both regarded me with suspicion.

I remember one colleague in my doctoral program cornering me in the library, saying with disdain, "You are an evangelical, aren't you?" Had I said, "No, only a convicted murderer," I might have made her breathe a sigh of relief. I told her what I said in all my different contexts of studying and teaching: "I really don't identify with labels." Expanding my worldview throughout my academic life, I also retained some nonnegotiable core convictions. My training and studies humbled me, because I could see there are many ways of expressing truth and honoring others in the process, but I was also aware how quick we are to judge others and try to put them in a box so we can either dismiss or engage them.

In retrospect, I see how the NAME IT process applied to my faith journey. I believe that God invites me to care for people across the theological spectrum. When I have talked with friends, colleagues, and fellow students who consider themselves "across the aisle" from me, whether more conservative or liberal (to resort to labels), the process of building a relationship has been the same.

We can exchange ideas with, learn from, and be challenged by those not like us. To do so might even expand our heart for and understanding of the extent of God's love.

I Noticed that I often felt scared and defensive in new contexts, aware I would likely be misunderstood. As I got to know others who were wary of me, I was able to Acknowledge their fears were just like my own. They had been rejected or punished in their past for being "different" (either too orthodox or progressive). With that awareness, I could initiate Merging our truths, so we could create space for one another in order to Embrace each other in our difference. By Integrating this mutual appreciation and open space in our relationship, I invariably felt Thankful for the person and God's gift of leading us into relationship. Through that process, I realized I was no longer an outsider to every group, and I could help others who felt like outsiders to feel known and understood.

I became more comfortable with difference. There were times in my past when I feared that engaging with those unlike me meant I would compromise my faith. I realized I was acting as if my security in God were extremely fragile and I was entirely responsible for safeguarding its well-being. But Scripture changed my mind. In story after story, Jesus did not shy away from engaging with people unlike himself or those he disagreed with. Usually he engaged them with stories and questions. Even among the Pharisees, he knew the cries of their hearts, from Nicodemus to the proud Pharisee who prayed aloud in the temple. I felt liberated.

We can exchange ideas with, learn from, and be challenged by those not like us. To do so might even expand our heart for and understanding of the extent of God's love. In addition, if we cross over into others' worlds, they may be willing to enter ours. In relationship and dialogue, not confrontation, we may be given the opportunity to share what it is we believe.

For many years, I have been a part of our local Interfaith Clergy Fellowship, including serving as the president and a member of the executive committee. Working with and getting to know my colleagues from different Christian and other faith traditions has deepened my convictions. Through this work, along with my experiences as a student, teacher, spiritual director, chaplain, and therapist, I have come to realize part of my calling is to be a "bridge builder" to God and others, and for others to God. In that role, I need to create space for God in my own life and cross the bridge to God in prayer and service. An important goal for bridge builders is to call others to a rich reengagement with the needs of others, a greater sense of their call to help advance the kingdom of God, bringing hope to the lost, food to the hungry, and justice to the oppressed. As we do so, our sense that those who are different from us are "other" can be transcended.

NAME IT with God

My (George's) journey with God has had a lot of ups and down in it. In the weeks following September 11, 2001, I was pretty pissed off at God. I didn't understand why God allowed this tragedy to happen. I knew so many amazing people whose lives were destroyed for no apparent reason. It did not make sense. It did not seem fair or right. To make matters worse, in my outrage God seemed indifferent. When I prayed, I couldn't feel his presence. In my moment of greatest need, I felt God abandoned me. The silence did bad things to me. My doubts grew roots, and my fears magnified. In my pride, I figured if God didn't want to talk to me, then I wouldn't bother talking to God. I questioned whether God really existed? As the distance between us increased, I stopped paying attention and didn't attempt to engage. The gap separating me from God seemed enormous.

Looking back, the NAME IT process of repair started for me when I was attending one of countless funerals for fallen firefighters after 9/11. I'll never forget standing at attention in our dress-blue uniforms in a line of hundreds of firefighters (usually there were thousands, but because there were so many funerals, firefighters had to spread out to cover the multiple funerals occurring simultaneously) and watching a widowed wife walk by holding her three-year-old son's hand. The image of his crying face wearing his father's too-big firefighter helmet seared into my soul. My heart broke as I thought about my own son and wife while walking through this real-time nightmare. Standing in that anguish, I closed my eyes and reached out to God asking, "Where are you?" (Noticing both my pain and longing for comfort).

Immediately, I felt God's presence and the answer: "I'm here holding that widow's and little boy's hands." I realized God hadn't gone on a vacation but was sitting in their pain (Acknowledging God's moves). Although I mistook God's silence as indifference, I then knew God was choosing to engage in their immense suffering. As my awareness expanded to recognize that God and I both wanted the same thing, to come closer together (Merging two truths), I no longer felt alone. Instead of defiantly turning away, I faced God and was blown away to realize that my vulnerable God loves me so much that God is willing to show me God's broken heart. In that incredibly gratifying moment of connection, I experienced God's whisper reminding me of God's eternal promise, not to protect me from the pain of the low road but to be my companion wherever I find myself, especially in the low places (Embrace). Talk about perfectly timed love. I knew with certainty that not only was God holding that little boy's hand but God was also holding mine.

Prior to this tender moment of connection, I was mad at God for not rescuing me from my pain and fear. In my rebelliousness, I turned away. I misinterpreted God's failure to save me from the agony of this tragedy as God not caring. Quite the contrary, God cares so much that God is willing to sit in the hurt, sadness, helplessness, and hopelessness with us. Wow, that is unconditional love. Although God plays no part in the sin of disconnection and disobedience, God is willing to meet us in the darkness. God showing up for me on that dreary day when I was standing at attention proved to be a turning point in my life. As this transformative experience of love replaced my fears with hope, I wanted to pay it forward with others (Integrate). That experience started me down a path of trying to show up for others in their emotionally painful places. Instead of running into fires, I now wanted to race toward those who needed help in the devastation of disconnection. I am amazed and appreciative (Thankful) for how God uses my story to encourage others to embrace the opportunities found in every moment, especially in the bleak places where we'd never expect to find that response.

Who Do You Believe God Is?

In reviewing the scriptural witness, we believe

- people are fearfully and wonderfully made in God's image;
- God knows and has plans for our hope and future;
- human minds plan their ways, but God directs their steps;
- what others may have intended for evil, God will use for good; and
- relationships are at the core of our existence and therefore are places where we need to give our time and attention in order to survive and thrive.

God cares so much that God is willing to sit in the hurt, sadness, helplessness, and hopelessness with us.

No matter what trials we face, nothing can keep us from the love of God in Christ Jesus. These are faith foundational pillars for us in writing this book. They ground our interactions with others and invite us to hear their stories with the assurance that change and redemption are possible. We may not be able to change events, but we can decide to face challenges with others.

We invite you to take a moment to journal whatever thoughts or ideas come to mind in response to these three questions:

- Who is God to you?
- How do you see God?
- How does God see you?

We believe the answers to these questions have tremendous impact on how we view ourselves and live out our relationships. God as the taskmaster and judge may create obedient but fearful followers. But what if the divine presence in our lives is kind, loving, forgiving, and gracious? How might that change our view of self and experience of others? Is God disappointed in you, or does God's heart leap with joy at seeing your face? We believe the evidence is overwhelming that God desires our best and calls us to participate in bettering the world and deepening all our relationships. If we open up our eyes to see the world through God's eyes, then we can't miss God's universal call for true connection among all things.

Everlasting Communion

Jesus's life reveals how to not worry about the future or relive the past but radically engage in the present moment, and he wants us to follow in his footsteps. He invites us to join him in the highs of ecstasy or the lows of despair and promises to join us there. The wider the range of vulnerable feelings, the more points of contact there are for us to relate to God and one another. No matter how bleak and despairing the picture looks, we must never forget that part of the human heart is always alive and longing for connection. With every beat, the emotional heart is working to fulfill its duty of making connection possible. We just need to set it free to complete its mission. Every single moment, the choice that matters most is how we choose to spend our limited time. Do we invest our energies in solo endeavors or in relationships? Jesus's life example definitely highlights God's yearning for us to choose communion.

Christians use many terms for one of the tradition's central sacred acts—Communion, the Mass, the Eucharist—depending on the church tradition. However, most Christians would agree with the statement that sacraments are an outward visible sign of an inward spiritual grace. God's grace is imparted in these tangible elements of water, bread and wine, and the act of partaking them together. Whatever you believe about the communion elements themselves, the common becomes holy and something mystical happens. In the same way, God takes us ordinary people with common problems and transforms us into agents of change and healing. God, surprisingly, often uses our places of weakness or scar tissue rather than our strengths. We consume God's body and blood to help us be God's agents in the world. And so we pray, "Lord, take these common elements of our lives and relationships and sanctify them by the power of your Holy Spirit for your holy purposes, that

No matter what trials we face, nothing can keep us from the love of God in Christ Jesus.

we might do justice, love mercy, and walk humbly with our God. Amen."

We hope our readers will listen to their hearts and come home to the embrace of God's love. When our work on earth is done, we won't worry about our possessions or reputations. Instead, our last breath will remind us of what is most important, the quality of our relationships. Every relationship is filled with misses, failures, and disconnection. The hurts are inevitable. But when we learn how to turn back toward each other, then it's possible to find love anew. Lives well lived are filled with those moments of connection and repair with God and one another. The good news is we don't have to wait till our last breath, God wants to make those meaningful and redemptive moments today. The choice is ours; where we decide to invest our responsiveness and engagement determines the quality of our existence. Heaven, which is the perfect word to describe the beautiful state of true union, is available right now.

God's grace is imparted in these tangible elements of water, bread and wine, and the act of partaking them together.

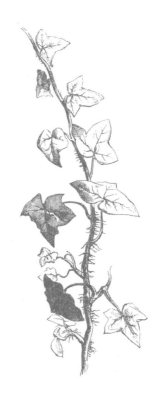

Notes

Chapter 1: Designed for Relationships

1. Matthew D. Lieberman, *Social: Why Our Brains Are Wired to Connect* (Oxford: Oxford University Press, 2015).
2. Rollin McCraty, *Science of the Heart: Exploring the Role of the Heart in Human Performance* (Boulder Creek, CA: HeartMath, 2015).
3. Michael Brown, *The Presence Process* (Vancouver: Namaste Publishing, 2005), 246.

Chapter 3: A Pathway to Repair

1. NAME IT process is inspired by Emotionally Focused Therapy (EFT) created by Dr. Sue Johnson. For more information, check out Sue Johnson with Kenneth Sanderfer, *Created for Connection: The "Hold Me Tight" Guide for Christian Couples* (New York: Little, Brown, 2016).
2. Debra Hirsch, *Redeeming Sex* (Downers Grove, IL: InterVarsity, 2015), 178–79.

Chapter 4: Navigating Romantic Relationships

1. Peggy J. Kleinplatz, A. D. Ménard, Marie-Pierre Paquet, Nicolas Paradis, Meghan Campbell, Dino Zuccarino, and Lisa Mehak, "The Components of Optimal Sexuality: A Portrait of 'Great Sex,'" *Canadian Journal of Human Sexuality* 18, no. 1–2 (2009): 1–13.
2. For more on our views of healthy sex and what gets in the way, see George R. Faller and Heather Wright, *Sacred Stress* (Woodstock, VT: SkyLight Paths, 2016), ch. 4.
3. C. S. Lewis, *The Four Loves* (New York: Harcourt, Brace, Jovanovich, 1960), 169.

Chapter 5: Finding Home in Our Families

1. Ellen Galinsky. "PBS's 'This Emotional Life': The Magic of Relationships," *Huffington Post*, July 9, 2010, https://tinyurl.com/y9ku9gel.

Chapter 6: Leaning into Loss

1. Hannah Hurnard, *Hinds' Feet on High Places* (Wheaton, IL: Tyndale House, 1975), 25.

Chapter 7: Discovering Community

1. Sebastian Junger, "How PTSD Became a Problem Far Beyond the Battlefield," *Vanity Fair*, May 7, 2015, https://tinyurl.com/ycdhdbfm.
2. Junger, "How PTSD Became a Problem."
3. Becky Ferreira, "Seeing Earth from Space Is the Key to Saving Our Species from Itself," Motherboard, Vice, October 12, 2016, https://tinyurl.com/y8kmm6ur.
4. Ferreira, "Seeing Earth from Space."
5. Henry Wadsworth Longfellow, *Hyperion and Kavanagh*, vol. 2 of *The Prose Works of Henry Wadsworth Longfellow* (San Bernardino, CA: Ulan Press, 2012), 405.
6. Harvey H. Guthrie, "What Does the Lord Require of You but to Do Justice, and to Love Kindness, and to Walk Humbly with Your God," EDS Now, October 23, 2015, https://tinyurl.com/ycphloy3.
7. Tom Rapsas, "Mother Teresa—On Why Loving Your Family Is the Most Important Thing You Can Do," *Wake Up Call* (blog), Patheos, May 2, 2016, https://tinyurl.com/yc88uydv.
8. American Friends Service Committee, *Speak Truth to Power* (Philadelphia: n.p., 1955), 68–69.

Chapter 8: Encountering God

1. Richard Rohr, Daily Meditations, Center for Action and Contemplation, https://tinyurl.com/y79zvwsa.

Bibliography

American Friends Service Committee. *Speak Truth to Power.* Philadelphia: n.p., 1955.

Brown, Michael. *The Presence Process: A Healing Journey into Present Moment Awareness.* Vancouver: Namaste Publishing, 2005.

Faller, George R., and Heather Wright. *Sacred Stress: A Radically Different Approach to Using Life's Challenges for Positive Change.* Woodstock, VT: SkyLight Paths, 2016.

Ferreira, Becky. "Seeing Earth from Space Is the Key to Saving Our Species from Itself." Motherboard. Vice, October 12, 2016. https://tinyurl.com/y8kmm6ur.

Guthrie, Harvey H. "What Does the Lord Require of You but to Do Justice, and to Love Kindness, and to Walk Humbly with Your God." EDS Now, October 23, 2015. https://tinyurl.com/ycphloy3.

Hirsch, Debra. *Redeeming Sex: Naked Conversations about Sexuality and Spirituality.* Downers Grove, IL: InterVarsity, 2015.

Hurnard, Hannah. *Hinds' Feet on High Places.* Wheaton, IL: Tyndale House, 1975.

Johnson, S., Sanderfer, K., & Recorded Books, Inc. (2016). *Created for connection: The "hold me tight" guide for christian couples.* New York: Little, Brown and Co.

Junger, Sebastian. "How PTSD Became a Problem Far Beyond the Battlefield." *Vanity Fair*, May 7, 2015. https://tinyurl.com/ycdhdbfm.

Kleinplatz, Peggy J., A. D. Ménard, Marie-Pierre Paquet, Nicolas Paradis, Meghan Campbell, Dino Zuccarino, and Lisa Mehak. "The Components of Optimal Sexuality: A Portrait of 'Great Sex.'" *Canadian Journal of Human Sexuality* 18, no. 1–2 (2009): 1–13.

Lewis, C. S. *The Four Loves.* New York: Harcourt, Brace, Jovanovich, 1960.

Lieberman, Matthew D. *Social: Why Our Brains Are Wired to Connect.* Oxford: Oxford University Press, 2015.

Longfellow, Henry Wadsworth. *Hyperion and Kavanagh.* Vol. 2 of *The Prose Works of Henry Wadsworth Longfellow.* San Bernardino, CA: Ulan Press, 2012.

McCraty, Rollin. *Science of the Heart: Exploring the Role of the Heart in Human Performance.* Boulder Creek, CA: HeartMath, 2015.

Rapsas, Tom. "Mother Teresa—On Why Loving Your Family Is the Most Important Thing You Can Do." *Wake Up Call* (blog). Patheos, May 2, 2016. https://tinyurl.com/yc88uydv.

Rohr, Richard. *Daily Meditations.* Center for Action and Contemplation. https://tinyurl.com/y79zvwsa.

Tronick, Edward. *The Neurobehavioral and Social-Emotional Development of Infants and Children.* New York: W. W. Norton, 2007.